"As African Americans, we take pride in our strength to withstand the stress of everyday life coupled with racism and other forms of oppression. However, pushing through the pain and stress is literally killing us. Rheeda Walker has delivered a much-needed gift in *The Unapologetic Guide to Black Mental Health*. Walker's practical guide centers on the lives and experiences of Black people to identify, understand, and provide language for our experiences with mental distress and pathways to emotional well-being. It is rare that I would recommend a book to parents, families, and mental health professionals alike. However, this is one such book. Walker translates research and best practices into an engaging and culturally informed style. This is a must-read for anyone interested in embracing hope and living one's best life."

—**Helen A. Neville, PhD**, professor in the department of educational psychology and African American studies at the University of Illinois at Urbana-Champaign

"In engaging and accessible prose, Rheeda Walker has created a vivid and forceful account of the experience of—to use her phrasing—living while Black, and of the sources of the psychological fortitude needed to sustain and develop self, family, and community. The concept of psychological fortitude is key to her ideas, and I believe that readers will find the concept both profound and useful in day-to-day life."

—**Thomas Joiner, PhD**, Robert O. Lawton Distinguished Professor of psychology at Florida State University, and author of *Mindlessness*

"While we're having a lot of conversations surrounding what's behind the suicides of young Black people, rampant self-medicating, and the importance of practicing self-care, *The Unapologetic Guide to Black Mental Health* provides the actual, necessary tools to look out for your wellness. That insight is provided in a voice that our community—young or old, woman or man—can understand and embrace. Rheeda Walker's work is right on time."

—**Victoria Uwumarogie**, deputy editor of the leading Black women's lifestyle site, www.madamenoire.com

"The transparency, expertise, and compassion that Rheeda Walker uses to navigate readers through a space in the mental health industry that has gone ignored by society is going to create emotional freedom and growth for generations to come. This is a brilliant and life-changing read that everyone should put on the top of their priorities list."

—**Devi Brown**, wellness expert, and author of *Crystal Bliss*

"In *The Unapologetic Guide to Black Mental Health*, Rheeda Walker not only provides an astute and revealing diagnosis of the pain and trauma we have suffered as Black people, but deftly guides us on a journey towards care and healing, rejuvenation, and self-affirmation. Walker demonstrates that Black mental and physical health is connected to a long history of racial terror, while reminding us that Black communities already have the cultural tools to achieve what she calls 'psychological fortitude,' our shield of protection and well-being. Using elegant language that easily switches between the conversational intimacy of a girlfriend, the knowing wisdom of an auntie, and the clinical experience of a professional, *The Unapologetic Guide to Black Mental Health* is also bolstered by historical examples and folk wisdom, popular culture references, and African proverbs. Walker has written a Black cultural tour de force; a robust and revelatory declaration that 'our very own culture can save us.'"

—**Jemima Pierre**, associate professor of African American studies and anthropology at the University of California, Los Angeles; and author of *The Predicament of Blackness*

"In her groundbreaking book, *The Unapologetic Guide to Black Mental Health*, Rheeda Walker speaks directly to Black people: her book helps us to understand how racism, daily stress, and socioeconomic factors impact our daily lives. She places our experiences in the larger context of our culture and our African roots, so that we can embrace the power that is within us: our resilience and fortitude. In doing so, Walker gives us recommendations for change, whether it be getting the help we need, or learning how to bring about emotional well-being."

—**Lily D. McNair, PhD**, clinical psychologist, and president of Tuskegee University

THE UNAPOLOGETIC GUIDE TO BLACK MENTAL HEALTH

Navigate an Unequal System,
Learn Tools for Emotional Wellness,
and Get the Help You Deserve

RHEEDA WALKER, PhD

New Harbinger Publications, Inc.

Distributed in Canada by Raincoast Books

Copyright © 2020 by Rheeda Walker
       New Harbinger Publications, Inc.
       5674 Shattuck Avenue
       Oakland, CA 94609
       www.newharbinger.com

Cover design by Sara Christian

Acquired by Ryan Buresh

Edited by Gretel Hakanson

All Rights Reserved

FSC
www.fsc.org
MIX
Paper from
responsible sources
FSC® C011935

Library of Congress Cataloging-in-Publication Data on file

Printed in the United States of America

22   21   20

10   9   8   7   6   5   4   3   2   1   First Printing

To Momma,
who insisted we could do anything that we wanted to do in life.

To Daddy,
who said, *"If life gives you lemons, make lemonade.*
If at first you don't succeed, keep suckin' 'til you do suc-a-seed."

Contents

Foreword

There are probably hundreds of "unapologetic guides for white mental health." Though they are not likely to be so titled, the content of these publications betrays the implied idea that mental health is the same, regardless of race. This book boldly and courageously challenges that assumption and speaks directly to Black people about unique issues that affect their mental health.

Reading this book is like being a Black person living in Minnesota or Rhode Island and suddenly awakening one spring morning and finding yourself on Peachtree Street in Atlanta with all the amenities of Black life and culture. In fact, the book is so engrossing that when I received a prepublication draft of it several weeks ago, I expected to use my old professorial skills of quickly skimming the manuscript for basic overview of its content and general direction, as I had done for thousands of student papers for several decades, but got trapped.

I started reading it, and skimming was not enough. Before I realized it, I had read the entire book, word for word, and enjoyed every minute of it. It was like sitting on the front porch drinking sweet tea with multiple generations of family/friends (with ambiguous lines separating the two) talking about mental stuff and handling life problems that we all knew were important but didn't have the words to say what needed to be said.

Rheeda Walker's "guide" is informative, professional, practical, useful, helpful, inspirational, motivational, personal, comical, relevant, refreshing, sacred, soul-stirring, and exciting. Though Dr. Walker earned a PhD in clinical psychology from a prominent (predominantly white) university and is a tenured professor at a demographically similar university, she is clear about who she is. Without apology, she affirms her identity as an African American woman who is committed to making her field of study and expertise relevant to the unique needs of her sociocultural community. These "needs" are certainly colored and shaped by the racial experience of being Black and female in an American, Judeo-Christian, patriarchal society.

This thoroughly Black-on-Black, for-Black self-help guide to mental health and well-being has the audacity to be addressed to the unique "psychological fortitude" and resources of Black people. It doesn't attempt to instruct others about Black people, but anyone who reads it will find such instruction because of its insightful analysis. It is primarily intended to instruct Black people about themselves.

As the title declares: It is an unapologetic guide for Black people to reclaim our mental health. It does not attempt to "normalize" Black people by distorting us as "simply" dark-skinned white people. It tackles the race and culture experience as both a poison and a healing potion for Black mental health. Rheeda Walker takes the radical approach of looking inside ourselves, our experience, our history, our culture, our Africaness for those strengths (fortitude) that have uniquely fed our still-unexplained survival, resilience, and even transformed evolutionary advancement as a consequence of overcoming odds that should have been lethal. She comfortably embraces the utility of evidence-based intervention while prominently invoking the "evidence of things not seen" as identifiable cause of otherwise inexplicable fortitude and transcendent capability.

The power that Dr. Walker demonstrates in this book is the power of embracing one's bilingual and bicultural abilities, or what the scholar genius Dr. W. E. B. Du Bois characterized as "double-consciousness." Such consciousness can be the source of inner tension or confusion if one is not certain about their identity. This tension with clarity gets synthesized into creative and expanded perception that generates the kind of readable, useful information that we find in this book. Again, she is unapologetic for using the African-centered method of science that freely moves between the empirical world of the Western scientist and the spiritual dimension that is included from the perspective of the African-centered scientist. Traditional African scholars experience no contradiction because they fully embrace the notion that "we are spiritual beings having a human experience."

Dr. Walker doesn't use this book as an opportunity for a secret conversation with her professional colleagues speaking in their encrypted professional jargon. She speaks as though she's speaking to her hairdresser, her cousin who is a single mother, her great aunt who still thinks that the PhD that has permitted her the title "Dr." means that she should be able to help her with that "misery" in her back. She also honestly confronts some of the cultural myths and distortions that are some of the poisons of mental health in the Black culture, such as fearing the stigma of admitting to being beat down by life or the idea of asking for help is a sign of weakness. "Crazy" is not crazy in a crazy world, and there is no shame in getting it right. She extolls the benefits of prayer and spiritual help but realistically identifies the limitations and the need of sometimes seeking supplementary interventions that are needed to deal with life.

This "guide" doesn't just describe the problem with weeping and wailing about toll taken by the problem, but Dr. Walker offers clear, useful, easily implemented suggestions of what to do. This book is a guide to self-help but simultaneously about how to get help. It speaks to the mind, body, and soul in the context of the African American life experience. Thank you, Dr. Rheeda Walker, for going where no woman has gone before to help Black people find reparation in ourselves. When we are repaired and reclaim ourselves, the world will find reparation through us, once again!

—Na'im Akbar, PhD

> Research Associate in Clinical Psychology (Retired)
>
> Florida State University
>
> Former President of National Association of Black Psychologists

CHAPTER 1

The Psychological Crisis Is Real: Let's Fight for Our Sanity Together

Do you tell yourself, like so many of us do, that Black people don't have time to feel anxious or get depressed? We have too much work to do. We have too many situations to manage at our children's schools; too many coworkers daring us to succeed; too much family drama. It takes everything in you to keep life going. The very effort to deal with your daughter, son, coworkers, supervisor, husband, lack of husband, or drama with friends leaves your emotional tank on empty. But you keep going because that's what we do.

Instead of paying attention to your feelings of anxiety or depression, or the signs of distress, you press forward. You remind yourself that Black people persevere. Even in the midst of a society of racial terrorism, you continue on—using your ancestral gifts.

Perhaps you have Maya Angelou's poem "Still I Rise" memorized to remind you of the reality that Black people have been despised, in part, because we seem to thrive no matter what. We tap into something special that has been cultivated for generations. When our ancestors struggled to live to the next day, endure inhumane treatment, and maybe…just maybe…be themselves without consequences, there was no time for emotional problems. After all, the book of Psalms says that crying endures for a night. Whether joy comes in the morning or not, it will be time to move on.

Evelyn, a grandmother who helps her adult daughter raise her kids as a single mother, recently described to me how overwhelmed her daughter is by her life. Evelyn remarked that she didn't recall struggling so much as a young mother because, "We just pushed through, you know what I mean?" I nodded, having heard this generational conversation often, especially in my own family. But then I encountered a statistic that sounded an emergency alarm for me. Some things for Black people have changed.

The Consequence of Our Lost Identity

Our cultural story, as a people who endure, is why I never imagined that Black people would become more at risk for suicide than white people. But then, in 2016, studies indicated that the suicide rate among five- to eleven-year-old African American/Black children had exceeded that of their same-age European American/white peers.[1] While suicide rates in fact declined for white children, they increased for Black children. This, in itself, implies an epidemic in Black mental health. As a researcher, I know that statistics can change, and I hoped that this one would. But in 2018, experts who track causes of death found the same pattern continuing.[2] Suicide for Black children is increasing. This is when I knew I needed to sound an alarm. While the alarm is for the broader community, I intentionally address Black women as the unyielding thread and vibrant energy that holds the culture together.

I am not a child psychologist and cannot articulate what could be going on in the mind of a seven-year-old who would have the desire and courage to take their own life. My primary area of expertise is with adults. However, I do believe that the emotional distress of our children is showing us that we are losing cultural values, which, for hundreds of years, have protected many African Americans from killing ourselves. I am writing this book because this is where we are—at the intersection of overwhelming, unaddressed stress and the absence of the cultural identity to help fix it.

Whether we identify as "Black" or "African American," people of African descent experience a complex psychological reality in the United States and in many parts of the diaspora. I use both labels to refer to people of African descent who reside in the United States. This seemingly interchangeable use of the two labels is intentional though the two are not the same. You may prefer to identify as "African American." Some of us identify as Nigerian, for example, and do not identify as African American, though some of us do. You should insert whatever identity is relevant to you with the understanding that our identity is not monolithic. There are many shared similarities among Black people, but differences exist. The similarities have important cultural meaning. This is why, like many others, I capitalize "Black." The capitalization is intentional. Robert Guthrie, imminent Black psychologist, indicated in his prefaces to both the first and second editions of *Even the Rat Was White* that capitalizing Black "seemed necessary" because it refers to a people and is synonymous with African American.[3]

Suicide Wasn't Supposed to Be Part of the Culture

Even if you do not go to church regularly, you may have done so at some point in your life. This is true for most Black people. As a result, church pastors tend to have a finger on the pulse of what it means to be Black in the United States. In a research study that was conducted in the early '90s, church pastors were asked their opinions about Black suicide.[4] They responded by saying that suicide was a "denial of Black identity and culture." To them, being Black is about struggle—there are no easy answers or easy outs. The overarching message from the pastors was that suicide is "a white thing" and that Black people are resilient because of the history of struggle and making a way despite being left out of mainstream society politically, economically, and socially. The author of this study concluded that this assumption about suicide was embraced throughout the Black community. I think that the church pastors who were interviewed were correct about suicide beliefs in the community then and they would be correct about the beliefs today. Nothing is so hard that a Black person could take his or her own life, right?

We assume that a weak or selfish person might kill him- or herself and that a strong-minded Black person would not do such a thing. Suicide is presumably not what Black people do. The accepted definition of "suicide" is "death from injury, poisoning, or suffocation where there is evidence that the person who died *intended to kill herself*."[5] Because we assume that Black people are resilient no matter the circumstance, no Black person would *intend* to die.

This is part of the cultural force that is driving our conversations about anxiety and depression underground. We won't talk about the persistent feelings of depression or the suicidal urges that result. We won't reach out for help because we stand together in denying our pain.

The reality of mental health challenges in my own family brought me here too. Can you imagine being the only psychologist in a large Black family? Just like many other families, we do not talk about the things that are right in front of us. We didn't when I was a child—though I can add that I did not know much as a child because, like you, I was not allowed in grown folks' conversations. As an adult, however, I know for sure that we still do not talk about realities that stare us in the face. It is one thing to endeavor to embrace a family member despite the fact that he hears voices. It is another thing altogether to refuse professional help and hope that the problem will go away with prayer and rabbit tobacco. Taking a vitamin or herbs and hoping for the best is not going to help a relative who is upset by the voices in his head. Things will not change unless we actually do something: find a competent professional, take medication as prescribed, and go to group therapy for support.

In the Black community, very few people feel that they have someone reliable and trustworthy to call. As a result, the interplay of stigma, limited knowledge, unexpressed pain, and lack of access conspires to keep many families from overcoming unnecessary cycles of hurt. It is time for a shift. It is time to have more honest conversations. If you are going to reinforce your mind, we are going to have to be honest about the problem at hand.

Psychological Distress Goes Unchecked

Imagine one of your more defeated days. Say it's a day when nothing is going your way, no one is helping you, ten people are trying to pull you in different directions, and you are sick of it all. Your children won't listen. You don't remember the last time that you had time to yourself, and there doesn't seem to be any peace in sight. Worst of all, you expect that tomorrow will be no different.

You might have a very quiet thought that things would be so much easier if you could go to sleep and not ever get up. Even with that thought in mind, you maybe cannot imagine life becoming so hard that you'd decide to take your own life. But people who die by suicide do not want to die. They just want their emotional pain to end.

When you are in such pain, you probably do not want to ask for help because, like many Black people, your pain doesn't register as a crisis. You are supposed to have the strength to handle whatever life throws at you, so you don't get help for yourself or reach out to help someone else.

Before you know it, you have a stroke, a heart attack, or an emotional breakdown or attempt suicide. Is it a suicide attempt if you have a heart attack? No, it is not, but it is a situation that could have been prevented. Perhaps you eat what you should not because some small part of you is ambivalent about whether your life ends or not. Our ongoing, unchecked habits will soothe emotional pain in the short term and shorten our life in the long term.

Recognizing the dire state of Black mental health may require that you reject what you have come to understand about what it means to be emotionally healthy. Just because you were able to get the boys fed and off to school with packed lunches and completed homework and get yourself to work with your hair done and clothes coordinated does not mean that all is well. You cannot articulate what it means that you can accomplish all of this yet feel so sad and empty almost all the time.

In this book, I will help you gain the language you need to explain what you see and how you feel, from a perspective that makes sense. I aim to share the reality of our mental health crisis and what I have learned about a possible path to Black psychological liberation and well-being.

The Relief of Honesty About Our Experiences

The belief that we can endure anything is both a strength and a weakness of our current culture. Those who are having the hardest time can be the least likely to ask for help because they are afraid of not appearing "Black enough." This happens on top of everything else that is causing pain.

A popular quote may have been misattributed to Harriet Tubman, but it says that she would have freed a thousand slaves and saved a thousand more if they knew that they were slaves. Whether she said it or not, many enslaved people in Harriet Tubman's lifetime undoubtedly thought that bondage was better than risking death for the unknown. This profound statement that people could not be freed because they did not know they were in bondage—even at a time when the bondage was pretty obvious—is inconceivable. But if the life and generation-changing physical bondage wasn't obvious then, the psychological bondage and its consequences are surely unrecognizable now.

The epidemic of not knowing that we are enslaved to insane circumstances has continued. Shootings of unarmed Black people on the streets are met with collective inaction. We cannot kneel together to protest infringements on our rights because we do not realize our power to change the system. Instead, we live in fear and anxiety that any day "that could be my son." Living an inauthentic life of "going through the motions," disconnected from others, is not your freedom. Denying your Africanness until it shows up in a multibillion-dollar comics' movie is not your freedom. Even if you have never set foot on the African continent, that does not mean that you are "just American." It is your connection to a shared heritage that will get you to where you are supposed to be. Before you get there, however, you have to be clear about where you are.

In some families, it is acceptable that "Auntie ain't never been right in the head." This may be true but does not prevent the family from doing more for her. Your family's actions do not have to continue to be the way they have always been. Perhaps it is too late for Auntie to be healed, but it is also possible for her to get better if the family stops hiding her away and seeks help for her instead.

This dynamic of secrecy and the layers of pain are pervasive in too much of the Black community. On the one hand, there is a culture of staying out of others' business or personal affairs. On the other hand, doing so limits options for getting support when it is needed. Add another layer of being perceived as weak—and getting help isn't worth the effort. Poor communication and unresolved hurt could be addressed if there weren't so many layers of pain. It's an ugly cycle, but it is one that you can begin to chip away at.

You Need Psychological Fortitude

Researchers, experts, those who provide mental health services, and those who receive mental health services all acknowledge the "mental" aspect of psychology. But this word triggers visions of being "crazy" and "out of control." It's inaccurate, but perceptions matter. Some may feel that they will be disregarded for a mental "issue," but there is something about the word "crazy" that is like throwing a rock at a bee's nest. I don't know how such an intense reaction came about. It just is. To overhaul our thinking going forward, let's use "psychological fortitude."

Others have referred to "mental fortitude" and "mental toughness" more broadly as a type of psychological resilience—resilience that is the ability to withstand, endure, persevere through, and recover from difficult situations. People of African descent in the United States and around the world (individually and collectively) need high psychological fortitude. You need so much more than mental health or "well-being" in this era of discrimination, invisibility, and psychological warfare. You need an impermeable web of protection for your mind.

Even if you do not use sunscreen regularly or at all, think about how SPF, or sun protection factor, works. Of course, you can get by without it, but the reality is that it is recommended to protect you from harmful UVB rays that cause cancer. It is true that we are less likely than white people to be diagnosed with skin cancer, but when we do get it, we are more likely to die from it. SPF protection is assigned different number values, such as SPF 15 or 50. The crude reason for the SPF number is that it tells you how long you can stay in the sun without burning when you are wearing a certain level of a product. Some people, depending on skin type, need higher SPF than others.

This may be true for you regarding your "PF," or psychological fortitude, needs. I will reference this throughout the book. It is not a one-size-fits-all phenomenon. Instead, what you (or your loved one) need depends on a combination of how much exposure you have to life stress, discrimination, and relationship problems and your internal mind and body states. Some people deal with life situations differently and can endure more than others. If you (or someone you care about) cannot take on as much as someone else, that does not make you either weak or crazy. You just have to prepare differently and live your life unapologetically for you.

Sunscreen is sometimes waterproof, but after a while, it has to be reapplied to be effective. You often forget to maintain your protection as you are constantly distracted with all of the things that you need to do. You are distracted by all of the people that you worry over. You are distracted by all of the things you do for others rather than taking time for yourself—taking time to sit, reflect, and think about what is important and how you can re-up your psychological fortitude. Similarly, with PF, we cannot rely on the same level of effort that protected us during certain times of our lives to simply remain intact. We must do things differently. We must "reapply" our protections. Life can be hard especially if you are ill-equipped to manage the challenges that will come. Just like your melanin does not fully protect you from the sun, one boost to your PF (such as a single getaway with girlfriends or an inspirational Sunday service) does not protect you from the serious and ongoing threats to your well-being.

In the Bible, where it says to "put on the full armor," I suspect that armor comes in different forms and types. We will revisit faith in chapter 8, but know that the armor or protection to your psychological fortitude must match the situation. Too often, we do the equivalent of taking an umbrella out in a hurricane. An umbrella is inadequate in storms when we should stay home and shelter in place. Yes, sometimes you need to cancel the commitment and stay home (or not make the commitment in the first place). Know also that just because what you've done in the past worked, does not mean that it will always work. Running around on five hours of sleep worked when you were twenty-five. Now that you are forty-five, get some rest. You will have to continually evaluate whether what you are doing is working for you in life or you will find yourself in a rut that is hard to escape. It is okay to keep the umbrella with you just in case, but don't assume that the same umbrella (or armor) will always get you to where you need to be at every stage of life or life situation.

Checking Your Psychological Fortitude

Use a psychological fortitude rating system as a quick self-check for how you are doing. I really like a 0-to-10 rating scale because you don't have to overthink it. You can do a quick evaluation of yourself or have others share a quick evaluation with you.

- A 10 rating means you feel phenomenal. Nothing and no one can break your spirit.

- A rating of 7 would pass as okay. You can recover from a very stressful day at work with just one glass of prosecco. You don't have the wherewithal to cook dinner, but you've had worse days and know that this too shall pass.

- A rating of 3 is not okay. You feel completely overwhelmed with life. It's probably nothing new. This has been going on for years. If one more thing goes left, someone is going to catch hell. You have no idea how you ended up here and no way to get out.

- A rating of 0 would be lowest possible level of psychological fortitude. Your circumstances are bleak, and you have zero desire to go on with life.

The beauty of this simple system is that the rating doesn't have to be perfect, but it works for two reasons: (1) it's easy, and (2) it gives you an objective impression of where you are at one moment or on one day *relative to* another day. If I, as your friend, know that you have been really struggling with your daughter and have been at a 4 on most days, but you are at a 6 after lunch with me, then I know that something has changed in a good way. You don't even really have to put a great deal of thought or conversation to it if you do not want to. It's a number.

The US Surgeon General's office refers to mental and emotional well-being as "essential to overall health."[6] People who have solid PF can cope with life stress, work more effectively, and essentially accomplish their purpose in life. You may have difficulty recognizing your life purpose because of unrecognized and untreated depression or other emotional health challenges. Because life happens, everyone benefits from high PF. I hope to show that despite the historical and current predicament in which Black people exist, where "supernatural" emotional well-being seems necessary, we have at our disposal resources and tools to move ourselves and our loved ones toward the mental and emotional wellness that we seek.

I wish that it did not have to be the case that Black people must have some type of magical ability to do well. Until things change, however, this is the reality. Much of the fortitude comes about by having a positive sense of what it means to be of African ancestry, as I'll explore in the coming chapters. One of my graduate students found in her investigations that identity may be related to having a sense of purpose. If our identity has been hijacked to suggest that we ain't never gonna be nothing, it is of no surprise that many of us are locked away in psychological prisons. Think about the amount of time that you spend in spaces where you are invisible or not heard or where you have to "contort" yourself or your hair to fit in. This demeans who you are as a beautiful spirit. Let us instead armor up, reinforce our individual and collective PF, and get clear about where we are, and more importantly, where we are going.

We've Survived...Together

I'm inclined to believe that our ancestors had something important that we're more likely to neglect today—they had each other. Historically, you have had to make your own way so many times that you see it as part of who you are. Your ancestors endured chattel slavery, rape, beatings, lynchings, Jim Crow laws, separate and unequal schools, housing segregation, and outright terrorism. Though previous generations were forced to give up their names, adapt their culture, or die fighting captivity, there was always some connection to the culture. There was nothing about the culture that said "minority."

It's not helpful to refer to yourself as a minority. If you want to be a "racial" minority, then fine, but please stop being "a minority." Words have meaning, and "minority" conjures up realities of being "less than." Some would argue that it's about being fewer in number, but people of color have always outnumbered white people in the world. In California, people from Mexico and Central America are already the numerical majority. In any case, if you're Black or African American, say that. Minority is not an identity unless you would like to perpetually see yourself as less than other people.

The earliest generations knew that they were African. When mothers and children were sold away to other plantations, new mothers stepped in for the motherless, and others consoled the grieving. Africans survived *together* under horrific conditions. This mind-set of survival was passed on from generation to generation.

When recent generations were enrolled in segregated schools, they were taught by Black educators who instilled a sense of pride in their young Black minds. Black people, who did not have much, lived in Black neighborhoods full of Black families who exhibited a proud sense of what it meant to be Black or Afro-American or Negro. You may have grown up in a situation where your grandmother, aunts, and cousins were a short drive or even short walk away.

We were once very clear about who we were and what our collective goal was—survival. And by "survival," we understood that individual survival necessitated survival of the community. Even when we became people who were in bondage, we knew this. Common faith kept us going. Families that were separated merged with new families. African American Vernacular English emerged so we could communicate.

These cultural evolutions provided a buffer that you may now be missing in the quest to fit in to "mainstream" America and achieve "upward mobility." We have lost so much of our prideful identity that, in the past, kept us going despite the heinous realities. It mattered less what *they* said and did because we knew who *we* were.

In modern generations, your parents sacrificed so you could have more than they had. They did this for you and not for themselves. It may be unreasonable and unfair for you to have the same expectations of yourself to work hard and take care of the community that your great-great-grandmother had for herself. She likely had more sisters and reliable mothers at the church than you have access to now. You may have financial resources, but unless you can use those resources to relocate your "village" to raise your children, you are indeed doing more with less.

The Price of "Independence"

Your cultural buffers, including family dinners, beliefs about what it means to "be Black," and the overall sense of interconnectedness, have likely eroded. Somehow, we have gotten in our minds that we can get by on our own. It is a symptom of the "me, myself, and I" of mainstream society.

Even if your mother was a single mom, she likely raised you in the same neighborhood where she grew up, surrounded by play cousins and other extended family. Your mother raised you to be strong and independent, so you went off to college and eventually accepted a lucrative job opportunity about eight hundred miles away from your old neighborhood. After some time passed, you became a single mom. You had no idea that it was so hard. Sometimes you feel like a failure as a mom, but you have no choice but to stick it out. You work your day job at the office and your night job at home with your little one, praying that things will get better one day soon.

One of my favorite memes says, "It is hard being a woman. You must think like a man, act like a lady, look like a young girl, and work like a horse." For Black women, add "fight for your sanity like a mixed martial artist." You want to work longer hours like your colleagues, but your responsibilities at home simply do not allow it. As a result, the boss conjures up "justifications" for why you won't get the promotion. Your mom visits on occasion, but it is simply not enough to offset everything that you have on your plate. It is time for change, but it's hard to even know where to begin. Meanwhile, the best thing that you know how to do is "never let them see you sweat." You press on, hoping that better days are ahead.

If you are fortunate enough to live near your children's nana or big mama or multiple aunties and uncles, you are most fortunate. You can call on them when you need them to pick up your children from school, take them to soccer practice, and teach them life lessons. If you can count on your neighbors to help "look out" for your children, this is also part of the village mentality that was integrated in the culture. If you get to be the favorite "auntie" for your nieces and nephews, your life is even better for it. Everyone has a role to play. If it is feasible for Grandma to stay at the house rather than going to "a home" for old folks, she too has a role to play.

We Have the Ways Forward Already

What I have found is that those who have a sense of spirituality and are connected to what it means to be Black in a positive way are less likely to consider suicide than those who do not have a positive sense of their cultural identity. I am not exactly sure why that is, but I have my suspicions that are based on my own research and that of others.

In one study, I found that African Americans who believed that God was in control of life were less likely to consider suicide.[7] I suspect that if you believe that God (and not you) is in control of life, that means that you do not have the option to take your own life. I am not suggesting that Black people do not experience hopelessness. Note that some age groups have relatively high suicide attempt rates. However, I am suggesting that some will experience significant hopelessness but not see suicide as a solution.

In another study, I found a direct connection between culture and the type of religious or nonreligious coping that African Americans use.[8] In this study, African Americans who relied on their own ability rather than prayer or other religious activity were more likely to consider suicide. Not surprisingly, those who relied on their own ability were also more likely to report Eurocentric beliefs. That is, there are ways of experiencing the world that are consistent with a more *African-centered* approach or a more *Eurocentric* approach—spirituality and faith in that which cannot be seen is Africentric. Materialism and competition are more Eurocentric. Those who consistently disconnect from spirituality and African-centeredness seem to be increasingly at risk in our society. The increasing suicide rates for Black children, teenagers, and young adults may reflect a cultural shift away from spirituality and positive cultural identity and thus, the imminent breakdown of psychological resilience in the Black community.

In chapters 7 and 8, I talk about the cultural and spiritual guideposts that have protected many Black people from suicide in more detail. If we consider suicide to be the end of the emotional distress spectrum and we know (at least suspect) that our cultural identities and spiritual connectedness have "saved" a number of us from the brink, we ought to also consider their power to help with lesser, more common forms of mental and emotional dis-ease, such as anxiety and depression.

It may, on its face, seem too simplistic to imagine that our very own culture can save us. But it has, and it can. The good news is that in the following chapters, I offer solutions that are already within your reach, hidden in plain sight, or perhaps even still a part of your family traditions that need only to be put back in place and reinforced.

PART I RECOGNIZE SERIOUS THREATS TO EMOTIONAL HEALTH AND LIFE

CHAPTER 2

What You Can Do If Death Seems Like the Best End to Pain

I have seen how uncomfortable the topic of mental health is. Whether it's everyday people who I talk to about my work, student psychologists in training, or even, at times, among my professor colleagues, everyone expresses unease. Believe me, if those who are trained to work with people in crisis have their own fears, I can imagine all of the thoughts that could go through your mind as you read this. Here are the most common forms of resistance that I hear to possible emotional health problems:

- "I'm fine. I'm just tired and need to get some rest."

- "My brother is just going through a phase. He'll be all right."

- "I don't have time for this; I have my own problems."

- "She can't be that bad off. I'll check on her later."

- "Don't try to get in my head. It's not that serious."

Given resistance to discussing suicide, the urgency it presents, as well as the crisis we are facing, I want to address it first thing in this book. I wouldn't be surprised if you would rather skip this chapter altogether and move on to more inspiring solutions. Even health professionals gloss over, or skip, suicide-related topics. They do not ask their patients and clients if they are thinking of suicide because it will make the patient uncomfortable. Unconsciously, however, they may not want to know if a person is thinking about suicide because they do not want to be embarrassed if their observation is wrong and the patient is offended.

Imagine that you disclose to your white doctor that you have been feeling down. She responds with a series of questions, including, "Have you had thoughts of hurting yourself?" You may wonder if she understands that suicide is for white people. Even if you have considered suicide, you deny it. However, if you have been thinking about suicide, you will benefit from answering the doctor's questions honestly. What is more important than writing a prescription or telling you to get some rest (which she may do) is the need for her to take the time to determine if you are in danger. Avoiding the truth of your distress will not help.

Most of us avoid situations that we fear and that make us uncomfortable. This can be true also for professionals who do not want to be perceived as incompetent. We conduct our lives accordingly. We sometimes do not want to acknowledge what we are truly feeling; it's also hard to experience someone else's pain.

This could be true because you are overwhelmed with navigating life. You do not know where to begin to help yourself or someone that you care about, but you can begin by being honest about your fears and perhaps by learning some terminology that shows there are levels to suicide risk. Given the language and a better understanding, you can begin to address your fears and help someone else along the way.

Suicide Language Explained

Suicide experts describe a range of suicide-related realities that exist from less to more serious:

1. *Suicide thoughts* or *ideation* are the ideas about ending life. For someone to wish that they were dead or so tired that they don't wake up is passive suicide ideation. If anyone is thinking about suicide, they are not in a good place, but they are also not likely to be in imminent danger of dying.

2. A *suicide plan* marks the next level of seriousness. It occurs when someone is so frustrated that they come up with a plan

for how to end their life. The preliminary research would seem to suggest that Black people are more likely to be impulsive and less likely to have a plan, but I think that we are simply less clear on the details of how we might die. If anyone knows how they are going to die, this would seem sufficient for a plan.

3. *Suicide attempts* are the hardest to define but if someone does something to intentionally end their life, they have made a suicide attempt. Attempting suicide is serious because people who have had suicide attempts are more vulnerable to attempting suicide in the future. They need more support for weeks and months down the road—support with whatever they are dealing with and confidence that they are not alone.

Even if a person survives an attempt, they may not be "okay." The circumstances that led to the attempt may have gone away temporarily. People rallied around them for a little while. But once they are "back on their feet," they are back to being alone with their troubles.

Say your son felt that he had no way out after his first love broke up with him and taunted him on social media. He hid his thoughts about suicide and made a plan to die, but never went through with the plan because you realized that something wasn't quite right. A serious problem emerged, but you intervened. Suicide risk is not 0 percent likely on one day and then 100 percent likely on the next day. Unaddressed problems often escalate, but that does not mean that you cannot step in at just the right time. Any time is the right time if you suspect a problem.

Fears are understandable, but they cannot keep you from paying attention, as suicide thoughts and actions could be hidden in plain sight. So let's take the first step to move past the fear. I know that is easier said than done, but I can guide you into thinking about suicide differently. By the end of this chapter, you will be more prepared to help yourself and someone you love. Keep in mind that people do not "commit" suicide. Suicide is not a crime just as cancer is not a crime. Some have *died by* suicide. Using language such as this will help communities dial up more initiative for those who need support.

Overcome Your Fear of Acknowledging Suicide Risk

You may fear that if you admit someone may be thinking about suicide, the person will die and you will have failed—or worse, you somehow contributed to the death. This is understandably terrifying. If you admit someone is thinking about suicide, you feel responsible for saving him or her.

Perhaps you cannot understand how someone could kill him- or herself. Maybe your own thoughts of suicide have snuck into your mind. The thoughts would have scared you because the rational side of you cannot imagine taking your own life. It might be easier to manage your fears with denial, but you do not have to stay in a place of denial.

If you know someone who may be suicidal, or if you ever encounter someone in the future and have your suspicions (which, given the statistics, you are likely to), I'd like to share with you what I tell my students so they won't be paralyzed with the weight of saving a life. When someone decides that they want to die, there is nothing that can be done to stop that person. Nothing. It is a jarring statement. Most students stare at me as if there is a punchline, but there isn't. Rather than saving a life, my only responsibility is to ask questions and be a good listener for someone who is feeling this degree of loneliness or overwhelming hopelessness. By holding this perspective, you can move out of fear and into a place of action.

If you tell yourself that you must keep your sister from killing herself, you should be scared. That is an enormous responsibility. Instead, when you see your responsibility differently—to connect with her, let her know that you care, and not be judgmental—you will be able to take steps forward to help. Consider these ABCs of support instead:

- *Assume that you can help.* Being present and available makes a difference for someone who feels isolated. It does not matter that you are not her best friend or that you haven't talked in months or that you don't share your "personal business." Being present shows that you care. That means more than you know.

- *Be a good listener.* She needs to connect even if she does not realize how much. You do not have to talk about her frustration of failing at work and in marriage. You can acknowledge that she is going through a tough time and that it is understandable. If you can, tell her about a time that she helped you personally. Share with her what you value about her but perhaps haven't ever shared. Evidence that she matters will go a long way.

- *Cancel your judgments.* You *cannot* be helpful if you're being judgmental, asking why she feels the way that she does, or trying to convince her that things aren't so bad. I cannot imagine a scenario in which your personal values would help. Other people's judgment is exactly why she does not talk about her problems. If you know that you like to judge people and tell them how to feel, revisit the previous bullet point, *be a good listener.*

The reality is that no one can keep anyone from doing something that they want to do. It is as plain and simple as that. You do not have to put pressure on yourself to make someone think the way that you think or do what they do not want to do. You only have to be a good listener and understand your loved one's experience from her perspective and be available to help when needed. Use your ABCs.

Know When Something Is "Off" in Yourself or Others and Be Ready to Act

The first step is not to be fearful of suicide and to face its reality. The second step is for you to let your knowledge of yourself and your loved ones tell you when things are "off." As difficult as it is to do, you have to realize that suicide is a real option for your loved one in emotional pain.

For your part, those who are nearest to you need to be able to ask if you are okay and want to hear the answer if you are at risk for taking your life. Also, you need to be ready to ask someone how they're doing *and* hear the painful truth. Suicide is a puzzle that friends and family members are more likely to assemble after a suicide death. Instead, we need to learn how to stand with the disconnected person in her troubles.

I was struggling recently with an overwhelming frustration. It did not help that I had just received some really bad news. I was in a funk. A friend asked if I was okay, and I said "yeah" without any thought. Fortunately, I have friends around me who don't take no for an answer. You know these people. They can be annoying at times—especially when you would rather be left alone. But we all need these kinds of people in our lives. We need them for the times when we cannot be strong and brave on our own. This friend said, "No, are you *really* okay?" Her question made me think about how I was doing for a moment. I mumbled some kind of answer, and she told me in a matter-of-fact way that I did not sound like myself. In that moment, her serious tone of voice snatched me to the reality I was not okay and needed some support through a tough time.

I appreciated that my friend cared enough to ask how I was and to not just let it go when I tossed out a deflective response. It would have been so easy for her to take me at my word and move on. It also *could* have been easy for me to get defensive. I could have said, "What—do you think I'm suicidal or something crazy like that?" We do that sometimes. We lash out at those who care about us. Doing so pretty much guarantees that the next time a friend hears something from us that isn't quite right, she won't say a thing to challenge it.

Be careful about how you hide yourself from people who care. Your hiding could set up a life-or-death situation whereby you are in need and there is no one left to help. Value the "don't take no for an answer" types in your life and try to appreciate their attempts to help.

You can follow through on your concern for people by insisting on the truth about how they are. After a while, they will begin to do that for you. We all want to be of use to those we love. Begin by acknowledging that your friend is in a stressful time of life that would be tough for anyone to overcome. Avoid saying, "It's gonna be alright." If she is fighting battles on multiple fronts—aggravation at work, fiancé problems, money problems—she is overwhelmed and cannot yet see the light at the end of the tunnel. If she is overwhelmed, she may not be able to figure out what seems obvious to you. And if she does, she may feel paralyzed to make any moves to address the problems. You can figure out the smallest step and help her go for it. Also, let her know that you are concerned about her and that you are there to help. Figure out anything that you can do to take the weight off her shoulders.

You can make yourself available by offering an alternative suggestion of something to take her mind off of things. You also may be going through a stressful, but not terribly difficult, time but you have to eat, right? If possible, ask your friend if you can meet up by her job for lunch. You do not have to mention that you think she is overwhelmed with life and on the verge of an emotional crisis. Your only task is to offer a time-out. We can all use an occasional time-out. The goal is not to problem solve but to offer a bit of respite from the day-to-day grind. Don't bring up the stuff that you know is bothering her. Talk about you and your stress, especially if this is something that you would not typically do. Invite her to get a massage with you—tell her that you want to try out a new place and don't want to go by yourself. Then, find the new massage place because you deserve a respite too!

Be Kind and Acknowledge Emotional Hurt

If you are thinking about suicide, but no one sees you when you are down, no one will suspect that you need help. So, over and over again, you will find yourself alone in your struggle—with no one reaching out and perhaps even no one to reach out to.

This sense of isolation is common for people at risk for suicide in general. My research team reviewed suicide notes that were written by people from various racial and ethnic groups, including African Americans. One theme that stood out in the notes is that no one around them knew the extent of their pain. Given the frequency of suicide death, you may personally know of someone who died by suicide. If you have not engaged in your own research to understand suicide, you may have decided that they were weak or selfish in a way that you did not know. Perhaps you adjusted your impressions of the person rather than realizing their pain. If you think nonjudgmentally about what you knew of their life, could you accept that they must have hidden an *enormous* amount of pain from the people around them? By now, you have managed their suicide death in a way that makes sense to you.

If you are hiding your own suffering and overwhelming frustration, it is time to strategize for help:

- If you like to overthink things, take baby steps. Schedule a time to schedule the phone conversation for when you plan to ask for help. Set a reminder on your phone if you must.

- When asking for help, be specific about what you need: Ninety minutes to watch your three-year-old on Saturday while you take a time-out? Someone to go shopping with you to look for an outfit for your anticipated job interview? Be as specific as possible.

- Create a list of specific requests that you can ask of those around you to relieve some of the burden or make a list of very small steps that you can take to reach a necessary goal. Think, *I will watch five minutes of this how-to video during my lunch,* rather than, *I have to organize my whole office next week.*

- If it helps, think of something that you can offer in return so you do not feel that you are taking advantage of your helper. Alternatively, you can plan to do something nice, like pick up a bouquet of flowers for her. Show your gratitude in a way that doesn't put you out financially.

- See this is an opportunity for you to be authentically you— strugglin' and all.

Be Your Own Cavalry or a Calvary for Someone Else

Unless you have lived under a rock, you have heard of "flu season." I find myself wondering when suicide will get flu-level treatment. Each year there are about forty thousand deaths due to suicide and hundreds of thousands of hospitalizations due to self-inflicted injuries. For the flu, there are also hundreds of thousands of hospitalizations per year. Annually, my son's pediatric nurse calls us when the flu shot is available. There are signs at every drugstore and persistent advice for the young, the elderly, and everyone in between to get vaccinated. The calls and alerts are part of a public health campaign to save lives. If someone dies prematurely and not by natural causes, but due to some cause that they could have prevented, that is a public health problem.

There is no vaccine for emotional pain. However, the numbers of people who die by suicide each year suggest that suicide should be treated the same as other public health problems. Instead, we are a long way from devising a plan to prevent a mental health crisis among the most vulnerable. To add, hardly anyone would classify you as "vulnerable." By society's standards, you are presumed to live a comfortable life in which you can go anywhere you need to go and get whatever you need. Even when help is readily available for those who go through a mental health crisis, there will be no public health campaign for you to help you meet your emotional health needs as a *strong* Black woman.

There is a disturbing belief in Black folks having a higher threshold for pain, such that we are presumably able to withstand more pain than white people.[9] Consequently, even some doctors and nurses are less likely to provide treatment for Black people compared to white people. One study found that when we get pain medication, we get less of it, and have to wait longer than white people to get it.[10] This is true even in hospice, though the whole point of hospice is to rest peacefully during the final stages of life.

My point is this: the cavalry is not coming to help you. You are your cavalry. It's time to get your own self in gear. If you must, cancel your Netflix subscription so you can take an active role in taking your mind, health, and strength to the next level. You don't have to wait until tomorrow to take a small step today. When your cousin died suddenly a few years ago, you realized how short life can be. You were so shaken that you promised you would do things differently in your own life and for your children. That lasted about three weeks perhaps because your goals were too ambitious. Training for a marathon was never going to be your thing, but you can set reasonable goals like these:

- Take a twenty-minute walk each day if you schedule it at a time that makes sense. Set a timer on your phone. If you live in the South, walking outside for twenty minutes at lunchtime in July is not what you want to do, but if you think about it, you can figure out a plan that makes sense. Walk down the hallway of your building for a few laps. Decide on a route that won't take you past the chattiest woman in your department.

- Set a yearly reminder to schedule annual exams for you and each person in your household—and put all exams on your own calendar.

- Ask your most reliable and loving friend to chastise you when you're hemmin' and hawin' about seeing a professional when you feel down.

- If you're concerned about someone, but can't seem to find the right time to express it, send a text now that says, "When do you have seven minutes to chat?"

- While you're away from Netflix, take time to make a list of SMART goals for yourself. SMART goals are specific, measurable, attainable, realistic, and time bound.[11] Rather than saying, "I want to be healthier," make a plan to limit your fried foods and sweets to weekends only for the next thirty days. If thirty days is unrealistic, set a more achievable goal…like three days.

Put Suicide Risk on Your Radar

When it comes to conveying how dangerous any situation is, language is essential. Without the right language, we are much less likely to act and more likely to avoid confronting risky situations. Having the right language is important in so many aspects of our society. For example, many people live in hurricane zones and struggle with the warning systems. It is hard to know the difference between a "watch" and a "warning," and even harder to know what to do when a storm is upgraded to a higher category.

I didn't memorize the differences for watch versus warning until I was well into adulthood. The hurricane analogy is vivid to me because I live in Houston. During Hurricane Harvey, one of the most devastating storms to hit the United States since Hurricane Katrina, news reports anticipated the storm would be "catastrophic," but I had no idea what that meant or what to do about it. Is the wind going to be the most devastating part of a storm? If so, I may need to board up my windows. Or will the storm bring extreme flooding? If so, the only thing I can do is evacuate. The bottom line is that the warnings should be interpreted and broken down in a way so as not to further confuse you and also to direct your responses. With an impending hurricane, just tell me if I need canned goods for a week and a camping stove or if I need to go to the gas station and fill up extra cans.

Those of us who are professionally responsible for evaluating suicide risk have language to articulate circumstances for less or more severe risk. Perhaps because this type of language rarely gets to the public, you are less likely to know if your niece's thoughts of suicide are a "cry for help" or if she really needs help. Speaking of which, it is never okay to say this about someone, as it is dismissive. If someone is doing something to get attention, it would seem that they are in need. They may not be in crisis, but they are nevertheless seeking something that they do not have. You do not want to wait until they are in crisis.

My colleagues and I published recommendations for clinicians in training for how to respond and what to do based on risk.[12] Unless you are a professional, it is best for you to contact a professional for evaluation. I will attempt to show you how risk can escalate and how your behavior can change. You don't have to go to defensive readiness condition, DEFCON 1, because someone that you are close to is thinking about suicide. However, you do want to be proactive in addressing mild, moderate, and serious concerns. Here, I describe a few scenarios that you can consider. They are not comprehensive, but instead provide an illustration of how risk profiles can differ.

Mild risk scenario. Your single, twenty-nine-year-old brother recently lost his job and has been saying for a few days that he might be better off dead. He does not have a plan to die. He does not own a gun and is actually uncomfortable around guns since your cousin was accidentally shot when you were kids. He wouldn't kill himself because he has too much to live for. He absolutely adores his three-year-old daughter. He is going through a rough spot, but he tends to bounce back from adversity. He doesn't go to church, but he believes in God. You can be a supportive ear to your brother. Acknowledge that he is going through a tough time. Remind him of his strengths and things that he does well. Check up on him each day to see if anything changes, such as he starts to feel hopeless about life and finding another job to support his family.

Moderate risk scenario. Your married, thirty-nine-year-old sister has been in an emotionally abusive relationship with her husband for seven years. They do not have any children. At times she feels hopeless about her future, whether or not she will ever have children and whether her career will ever be what she had hoped. It is not unusual for her to have a sad, depressed mood for weeks at time. She overdosed in what seemed to have been a suicide attempt less than five years ago. She only drinks socially and does not use any drugs that you know of, but she seems antsy these days. When you ask her if she is okay and if she has been having thoughts of suicide, she says to stay out of her business. Acknowledge that she has been going through a tough time and that sometimes it can be hard to know what to do. Ask her: "If you were to have thoughts of suicide, would you tell me?" Express your concern for her. If you've always had a "rocky" relationship with her, check in with her friends to let them know that you are concerned for her well-being and solicit their help in getting her out of the house more frequently if possible. Pay attention to any new or unusual behavior, as sudden or unexpected changes in behavior could suggest that she is in crisis.

Severe risk scenario. Your nineteen-year-old niece went off to college and is home for winter break. The adjustment to college has been very difficult. She is a kind person but was always a pretty anxious teenager who managed to get mostly As in school. Her sophomore year of high school was rough when she had some type of breakdown due to bullying. Your sister never told you what happened for your niece to end up in the hospital, but you suspect that she had some type of emotional breakdown. This semester, she failed a class and is concerned that she will never be able to get into a good graduate program. You suspect that she has been drinking pretty heavily. She found out over Thanksgiving break that her high school boyfriend was cheating on her with someone at his university. She told her mother that she wants to die. She does not see any reason to live. Your encouragement about God taking care of things falls flat. Your niece feels completely hopeless about her future and doesn't feel as if her life will ever change for the better. She says she just wants to die. If she has a plan and the means to die, the situation is dire. She needs action from those who care about her to be sure that she does not harm herself. Let her know that you are there for her no matter what. Make sure to remove or lock away any possible weapons or anything that can be used to harm herself, especially anything that she mentions in her "plan" to die. It can be scary to consider this, but she may need hospital admission to stay safe. There is a lot to think about. Consider calling the suicide prevention hotline at 1-800-273-8255 to get help thinking through what to do.

You do not ever want to minimize or be dismissive of suicide thoughts. If someone has had a life situation that they cannot manage and are feeling hopeless about the future, you want to pay increasing attention. Even if you do not see the big deal, if it is a big deal to them, that counts.

My motivation to dive into the hard topic of suicide with you upfront is to alert you to a serious but preventable problem. You can avoid driving over a cliff to an unnecessary death when warning signs have been posted to alert you to what's ahead. Then you can maximize your foresight rather than lamenting your hindsight. The rest of this book will help you know how to steer away from danger.

CHAPTER 3

Poor Diet, Neglected Health, Addiction, and Low-key Suicide

"Do you think someone is suicidal if they use drugs that they know will kill them?" It is a question with many layers. What does one really "know" when they desperately need relief from intense emotional pain? So much of our personal pain, family frustrations, and struggles as a community can be traced to unspoken and unresolved pain and trauma. But if you can't talk about overwhelming feelings so you can get help, I wouldn't fault you for using or doing whatever you can to make it to the next day...or hour. *However*, if emotional suffering is the seed to your binge-eating despite being morbidly obese and to your cousin's binge-drinking despite her bad kidneys, it's more than a moment of weakness or a bad day. Other experts are much less likely to say this, but I aim to bring attention to "low-key suicide."

If your decisions put you in a situation that could inadvertently lead to your premature death, there is an underlying problem that needs to be addressed. Life-threatening problems such as chronic health issues and drug or alcohol abuse are worsened by the urge to resolve pain and suffering without addressing core feelings. While we are at it, we can add homicide, the number-one cause of death for fifteen- to thirty-four-year-old Black men, to the list of preventable problems that plague the community.[13] Too many of our statistics are dire. We can begin to understand the enormity of the challenges and confront deadly obstacles as an informed community.

Suicide by Neglecting Physical Health

Do you take insulin for type 2 diabetes? If so, do you take your insulin, eat right, exercise, and monitor your blood sugar as is required to manage your diabetes? The odds are (sadly) pretty high that you will say no to doing some of these. If you have a loved one who isn't taking care of their illness, you are a witness to the issues that escalate already poor health.

I expanded my research beyond suicide to include diabetes because I have always been concerned about the connection between depression and physical health. People who have diabetes and other kinds of serious health problems often deal with depression. It is hard to manage a chronic illness like diabetes or high blood pressure when you are depressed. It makes sense that your mom could be feeling so low that she forgets to take her medication. But health neglect is not okay. When life is on the line, it is unacceptable to skip medication, mismanage serious health symptoms, and be a couch potato. It is self-destructive, but it is also part of the ongoing narrative. Here is some of the thinking that we have to change in our families and in our communities.

"It's not a big deal. I know a lot of people with (diagnosis x), and they're fine." This is a place where we have to stop comparing ourselves to others. Identical diseases can show up differently (and be deadly) in different bodies. We don't know what the other person is going through.

"The doctor is wrong." You're only thirty-four years old, but the doctor says you will need to take medication for cholesterol if you do not start managing your diet. You think the doctor must be mistaken, but is it worth it to take a chance if the doctor is right?

"Doctors are racist." You were referred to a specialist due to irregular bloodwork, but you didn't go. Your aunt died because racist doctors didn't help her in time. You may be right, but you can get a referral for a doctor from someone that you trust.

"High blood pressure just runs in the family." You inherited higher-than-normal blood pressure and cholesterol. Unfortunately, you were only assigned one body. It is your responsibility to take care of it.

"The way my mama cooks isn't good for me, but that's the only way it tastes right." Your mama's cooking is the highlight of your otherwise dull week. Maybe there are other ways to liven things up.

Serious but avoidable health problems could be just below the surface. Ignoring our bodies or pursuing habits that exacerbate and worsen health is one way that we slowly kill ourselves.

Suicide by Another's Hand

I do not absolve law enforcement of any responsibility in "officer-involved shootings" of Black men and women. Anyone who does not know the difference between a weapon and a wallet or otherwise kills an unarmed person should be ineligible for law enforcement. That's not what I'm here to discuss. We need to be aware of the many possible ways that a person who is ambivalent about life could die prematurely.

One of the first studies of "victim-precipitated homicide" was published in the 1950s, but a lot of the assumptions that the researchers made and what they actually found in the study are relevant now. The author of the study, Dr. Marvin Wolfgang, speculated that there are people who, for different reasons, provoke others to kill them.[14] They want to die, and they instigate their own murder. Wolfgang's research found that Black men accounted for a higher rate of victim-precipitated homicide than they did nonvictim-precipitated homicide—basically saying that Black men were more likely to die in situations that they instigated than they were to die in a situation that they did not instigate. Wolfgang's research suggested many homicide deaths may be due to suicide in disguise.

I highlight this preliminary research not to exonerate any perpetrator but to expand our thinking on why we lose so many young men to violence. You are more powerful to intervene early and support your loved ones with this information. Black children need a place to belong in this sometimes-alien culture that rejects them in subtle and not-so-subtle ways. Because of this, your sister worked hard to raise your nephew "right." She did her best to help him with homework and get him involved in sports even when she was underemployed and over-worked. She prayed for him and made sacrifices because she knew that this society is not going to cut her son any slack. Despite her best effort, your nephew's life began to fall through the cracks by the time he was a teenager. One night, you got the phone call that he'd been shot by someone with whom he had a bad history. He survived the shooting, but you knew that he was on a destructive path.

The research on victim-precipitated suicide is limited. Some would say that it is more "theoretical" and warrants a great deal more research to conclude that it really is a thing. Until we know more, and given the high homicide rates that affect our communities, it is worth it to consider warning signs that your loved one could be at risk for premature death at the hands of someone else:

- He does not believe that his life is worth much.

- He sees himself as a failure with little or no hope that his circumstances will change for the better.

- He often encounters stressful situations but lacks the problem-solving ability to deal with them in the most helpful manner.

- When asked how he sees his life, he seems eerily ambivalent about his future.

Whether your nephew is passively willing or actively wanting to die does not matter much. In either instance, he could die if you or someone that he trusts does not meet him where he is and support him emotionally. When you see these warning signs, refer to chapter 1 for more on what to do. So that you avoid communicating that he is weak, you might say to him, "For some young brothas who have been dealing with a lot, they think about ways that they could die." Ask if he's thought about this. It is not your best option to just hope that things get better. You cannot wait until he puts himself in a situation whereby his life ends at the hands of someone else. This is a hard truth. It is hard because it puts some responsibility on you.

Notice that I did not say this hard truth puts "blame" on you. Blame is about something having gone wrong and assigning responsibility for what went wrong. Your responsibility is to be honest about what you see in your loved one so you can help him before he ends up in a dangerous situation. Take off from work. If you can, cancel whatever commitments you have to support him and your sister. Detour from "business as usual" so he sees that he means more than anything to you. This might not be sustainable if he is not with or near you, but you can do your best to get him back on track.

If anyone who you care about seems to be struggling emotionally, you have to commit yourself to (1) knowing what is going on and (2) making yourself fully available. This would be a good time for the ABCs of support that I mentioned in the last chapter.

Suicide by Alcohol or Drugs

You likely know of at least one person who is killing him- or herself slowly with drugs or alcohol. To others, your spouse can seem perfect. He has accomplished a lot. He drives a nice car. He seems to have a great relationship with his children. In reality, he is a high-functioning alcoholic. Perhaps the problem is not alcohol, but he got caught up in the Vicodin the doctor prescribed for pain after he hurt his back. Shouldn't he be off of it by now?

You tell yourself that maybe he is actually okay since he is able to keep a job. Alcoholics and addicts can't stay employed, right? Pain pills can't be that big of a deal or the doctor wouldn't have prescribed them, right? Meanwhile, your life with this person isn't what people think it is. When people say, "You never know what goes on behind closed doors," they could be talking about your life. You don't know why your spouse spends his off hours mostly intoxicated. You reason that since he had a rough life growing up, his alcoholism is understandable. Even if you decide you should intervene, it's a tough situation because you understand that you cannot make someone do something that he does not want to do. You also do not have to live in denial or expect that things will change on their own.

Your loved one is killing himself slowly and perhaps in a way that seems more acceptable to him. But if his liver hasn't failed yet, it will. People who have alcohol problems are unable to quit even if they insist they can. Saying, "I can quit anytime," but not actually doing it is a sign of addiction. Whenever they try to quit, you see them physically shaking. They may seem much more irritable than usual, or they report feeling nauseous. These are signs of physical withdrawal from a serious alcohol-use problem. Locate a support group through your nearest National Alliance on Mental Illness (NAMI). We discuss this more in chapter 10, but with a NAMI (or other) support group, you can learn tools to support your loved one and, more importantly, to help yourself.

I realize that I may be pulling the rug out from under you. Denial may be the only strategy that you have for dealing with your life right now. I would understand 100 percent if you put this book away and came back when you are ready. Denial is actually a way of coping with situations that can be emotionally overwhelming. I get it. And I will say this more than once. It is only my intention to help you understand more about what is going on with you and those around you. Maybe you can help your loved ones, or maybe you cannot. I honestly do not know. What I do know is that you cannot begin to help what you do not know is a problem.

Even if you did not know that being in a drunken stupor every weekend is a problem for your high-functioning, nine-to-five husband, you are probably more likely aware that your sister who "gets high" most days of the week and has problems taking care of her school-age children is a problem. If you are dealing with addiction, it is hard for both the addict and their families.

At the root of excessive drug use is often some unaddressed pain or feelings of being unloved and unwanted, or feelings of emptiness and speculation that life isn't worth living—or at least it's not worth living without being high. The problem is not the drugs or the alcohol. The problem is the hidden pain and the denial of this pain.

If you try to force your husband or sister to address alcohol use without providing support for this deeper pain, you will get some push-back. People who use too much drugs and alcohol are not going to relinquish them easily. Imagine if your doctor told you to give up your two cups of coffee each day to help you fall asleep at night and better regulate your blood pressure. In this instance, a medical professional has advised you of the benefits of stopping something that you look forward to and count on to keep you going. How hard is that to do? I imagine you weighing the costs and benefits of the doctor's advice. You do so as if you have the medical insight to know better than the doctor. Now, assuming that you do not have a medical degree, you advise your loved one to take a break from the Hennessy that he looks forward to each day. Is there a difference really?

What you could do for your spouse instead is to be there for him as a nonjudgmental listener. Put yourself in his shoes. Drug users do not start out intending to disrupt their whole lives. They are coping with difficult circumstances the best way that they know how. The avoidance of pain is at the root of each of these three choices: drug addiction, health mismanagement, and vicarious homicide. There are many people working hard to escape their lives. You can use your ABC support skills no matter who it is and with what they are suffering. When, and if, they are ready to take the next step, they will find you.

Death Wishes Can Quietly Rule How We Live

You may still be wishing for me to move on from this part of the book. I wish that I could. The reality is that your availability to deal with suicide risk effectively for others will be limited if you are overwhelmed and thinking of ending your own life. You may just be hoping that you will end up in the hospital one day so that, for once, someone will take care of you and you do not have to work yourself to the bone. That would be so much more natural, and no one would know how truly exhausted you are.

You have tried journaling, spa time, shopping, and other means of escape and coping, but nothing seems to work. Life isn't getting better, and you question why you are alive. You have prayed and prayed and gone to church most Sundays, but any boost to your mood only lasts for a few hours after service. Some days, you wish that life would just stop.

We do not have to call it *suicidal*. If it will help you do things differently, we can call it something else—this condition where your psychological fortitude meter is on "E" and you have no desire to fill the tank. You have no energy to fight. You are only waiting for something to happen, though you have no idea what that something is.

You want to live and be happy, so you must not be suicidal, right? I do not want to be the bearer of bad news. I also do not want to scare you. I've already said that people who died by suicide did not want to die. They were just like you. They did not want to carry on, day in and day out, in this kind of pain. You may have had some or all of these thoughts. You no longer see the point in living.

And you do not want to burden the ones you love. Do you think that the people you care about will be better off if you were dead? I suspect they would not be better off. They may be really awful at communicating their gratitude, but their poor communication does not mean that they do not truly value you.

The good thing is that you do not have to mind-read with other people. If you want to be certain about whether they would be better off with you dead, ask. Don't ask flippantly. In preparation, make a list in advance of what you need for them to do to show that they value you. Choose the oldest or most mature person to ask your question. Tell them that you have an important question to ask. Ask your question. If they say that they would be better off, they have a problem, and it is no wonder that you have been miserable. Ask someone who does not have a serious emotional problem. The most likely response is that they would never be better off if you were dead. Then take out your list and tell them what you need from them—less criticism and ridicule, maybe? To take on some of your responsibilities? To commit to family time by scheduling activities? Asking for help will not come to you easily if you're accustomed to doing everything on your own. It is, however, something that you can do to get yourself out of a rut when you need to and elevate your PF.

Unnecessary Struggle

You might be stuck in thinking appearances matter more than addressing what's really going on with you. But actually, to elevate your PF, you may need to rid yourself of the artificial stuff, such as:

- advancement in a career you despise (where you don't get the respect you deserve)

- unaffordable shoes, handbags, and social events (pushing your credit card debt out of control)

- pursuit of compliments and admiration from others (though they don't even know the real you)

In the end, you feel even more isolated. You have carried the weight of your entire family on your shoulders at times, and no one appreciates how much of yourself you have sacrificed so everyone else can be their best selves. You used to feel resentful, but you have simply lost the will. You used to say that it doesn't matter, but now you are just numb, feeling like you cannot have the life that you thought you'd one day have.

You are not alone. You may not know how you arrived here, but you do not have to stay here. No one has to remain stuck, no matter how dismal the situation may seem. Keep reading this guide and, as you do, try simple steps toward change.

We are conditioned to "go big or go home." It sounds clever, but it's not practical. Small steps are anything that is different from what you would normally do. Would you typically eat a bag of potato chips when you are upset? Okay, leave six chips in the bag instead. If you often drink a bottle of wine by yourself on Friday after an impossible work-week, drink half the bottle or delay until Saturday to drink the whole bottle. Do something (anything) that is different from your usual.

You Are a Difference-Maker

If your loved one is considering suicide or seeking death by other means, they are having an emotional crisis that is marked by feeling like life does not matter and that things will never change. Because suicide is seen as unacceptable, so many of us do other things to sabotage health and well-being. The mind can play tricks on a person.

Our presence for each other is important. Demonstrating that you care no matter the mistakes or how much you disapprove of past decisions will mean more to anyone than you know. I can tell you this even if the person in pain cannot or will not.

Resilience in the face of adversity is both a strength and a weakness for Black people. Somewhere along the way, we learned that we can never be vulnerable. If someone seems to be suicidal, in any of the ways I have described, it does not mean that you have to "call them out" for what you see. You can be present and remind them that someone cares. Do for them what you would want someone to do for you when you are down or feeling like life is not worth living. Standing without judgment for someone who needs support is a strength.

The decision to accept your help, to improve their situation, or to follow the prescriptions afforded them for improvement is their decision to make and only theirs. You are not responsible for their actions or inaction. You cannot make anyone do anything they do not want to do. You are not responsible for their decisions or the resultant outcome. This is a difficult truth to accept, but embracing it will help you get past your own fear about suicide so we can face this crisis together.

CHAPTER 4

The Anxiety and Depression
Beneath It All

If you attend a church, your pastor may make reference to depression from time to time and how you ought not let life get you to the point of depression. My own pastor has said that people can be depressed "with a Bible on their lap." He says this to acknowledge that having faith in God or being a regular Bible reader does not inoculate you to depression. Even if you have never stepped foot in a church, someone has inevitably advised you not to "let life get you down."

Yet you may have experienced moments, days, or even years of profound and untreated depression. Even when people do not know exactly what depression is, it has come to be a mainstream topic. According to entries in the Urban Dictionary, an online site where large numbers of (presumably nonprofessional) people offer definitions of slang, words, and phrases, depression is "a living hell" where you wonder why you are alive. Another entry describes loneliness and isolation. Though entries in the Urban Dictionary are mostly submitted by young white men, the definitions likely reflect much of the sentiment of how everyday folks perceive depression.

If you are fortunate, you can recognize when you are in the middle of a depressive "episode" and take it seriously so you can give yourself a break rather than berating yourself for not being able to push through it. Because the feelings of depression, the low mood, the lack of interest in life, and maybe even the passing thoughts of being dead are so troubling, they mask the more common threat to your psychological fortitude—anxiety.

Anxiety and depression often co-occur, meaning that approximately 50 percent of people who experience debilitating levels of anxiety will also suffer from symptoms of depression and vice versa.[15] In this chapter, I'll explain how to recognize anxiety and how to undo beliefs that you may hold, like the notion that worrying all of the time is a normal part of being Black. We must begin to address important realities that have likely impacted you and the people you love—realities like how all of that worrying is making you physically ill and how you can choose to get professional help for debilitating anxiety. Many are unaware, but anxiety-related problems are the most commonly occurring problems in the United States. They are a real threat to our psychological fortitude.

Worrying Can Get Out of Hand

One of the things that intrigues me about chronic, ongoing anxiety is that a lot of people experience it, but do not recognize it as a problem. You may believe you're too strong to be overcome by emotional problems. Whether or not we acknowledge this temptation to view ourselves as superhuman, it's important to know when things are actually big problems.

It is normal to feel anxious about a job interview, or your kindergartener's first day of "real" school, or pulling off opening night for a major production that you have been working on for weeks or months. A certain amount of *short-term* nervousness that includes physical symptoms like nausea or shakiness is to be expected from time to time. Anxiety that goes on for years and years and is out of proportion to a situation, keeping you from your life goals, is *not* good.

You may have ongoing anxiety that centers on your frustration with your job. You worry about performance evaluations; you constantly feel undervalued and underappreciated; you feel you deserve a raise, but you worry that if you speak up for yourself, there will be consequences. You don't know the consequences, exactly, but you believe they exist. In this case, anxiety is about the fears that you have (of perceived consequences or potential confrontation) and what you do (i.e., avoid speaking up) to manage your fears.

Meanwhile, you find that you are also dissatisfied with multiple other areas of your life. You have been saying for five years that you are going to lose twenty pounds, but you cannot stay on any diet plan and end up beating yourself up because you should be able to control your eating habits. You do not have any serious health issues, but you figure that something must be around the corner given your family history.

When you are honest with yourself, you realize that you are so overwhelmed that it feels impossible to clear your mind even when you are in the shower. Really, when was the last time that you showered without thinking about what happened that day or what you needed to do the next day? Pay attention the next time you take a shower.

Despite everything you worry about, you cannot get yourself mobilized to do anything differently in your life. It seems just enough to push your way through to get up each day. It does not feel good, but you could not imagine that this way of life is something worth seeking professional help to shake.

There may be people around you who worry all the time about everything. Maybe your grandmother and mother worried constantly. Worrying and the aggravation that goes with it are a part of life—worrying whether to leave the job, leave the husband, leave the child in that school, or maybe even leave the country—these worries are surely a part of life. Unfortunately, they can be disruptive when the time comes to actually accomplish change in your life.

We neglect our emotional health the same way that we neglect our physical health, except that our neglect for our emotional health is far worse. We neglect problems until the situation is dire or can no longer be avoided. If you were to break your leg, you would see a physician right away because getting around on a broken leg would be really hard to do. Because emotional problems do not shut us down, we keep going despite the potential long-term consequences.

A few years ago, I experienced anxiety symptoms that were significant enough for me to make an appointment with my physician. I did not know that it was anxiety for sure. My first step was to rule out that

I was having a serious health problem. Though I was generally very healthy, I was already more than forty years old with a family history of high blood pressure and the other usual suspects—high cholesterol, diabetes, and so forth. I had been experiencing slight pain and tightness in my chest. After a few months (yes, I have been guilty of delaying care), I made an appointment with my primary care doctor, who chastised me for waiting so long to see her. At the appointment, she recommended several inconvenient tests that required long appointments, not eating overnight, and being in freezing rooms wearing thin gowns. I was not happy about these tests, but we had to determine if there was something wrong with my heart. I did not want to deal with the inconvenience given all of my responsibilities. I do not know of anyone who prefers to be inconvenienced. Who has time to sit at the doctor's office when there are deadlines at work? More importantly, what if you get bad news? You don't have time to deal with bad news.

While health exams may be inconvenient, you want to make sure that you are in good health and that any physical pain or discomfort that you are feeling is not a serious health problem. Inconvenience is not worth your life. I cannot underscore this enough.

"Worry" that is constant and showing up in your body as physical ailments should not be ignored. You are not superhuman. When you wait out your symptoms in hopes that they go away, even when they seem to disappear, there can still be a serious problem waiting to reemerge. Anxiety and the symptoms of heart disease and other health conditions can overlap. If you do not go through the physical examination and follow-up, you cannot have any confidence about the source of your physical symptoms. After my doctor ruled out physical health problems, she shifted to a different set of questions that I, in my professional experience, knew what the answers meant. So we then discussed whether I was experiencing anxiety symptoms and what to do next.

Signs That Anxiety Is a Problem

Have you ever been told that you make up things to worry about? Even then, perhaps you cannot seem to get your worrying under control. Before now, you may have accepted it as "who you are," but it is something that pokes big holes in your psychological fortitude raft.

If you can find anything to worry about on any given day, have a hard time being reassured about the thing or things that you worry about—even when you talk to others that you trust—and this has been your way of life for years, it may help to see a professional for a formal assessment. Mental health experts define the broadest form of anxiety as *generalized anxiety*, a persistent and excessive worry or fear.

It is understandable that you would worry about an upcoming evaluation for promotion at work or how you are going to help your daughter with her science fair project. These are understandable concerns. Generalized anxiety is a diagnosable and treatable problem that comes with a set of other problems, such as feelings of fatigue, problems sleeping, feelings of being "on edge," problems relaxing, problems concentrating, including having your mind "go blank," and muscle pain (that isn't accounted for by that new workout you started).

There are physical symptoms of anxiety that you may have dismissed but are connected to what mental health professionals call *panic disorder*. Have you ever had unexpected symptoms such as a racing heartbeat or the sense that your heart is skipping beats and shortness of breath, perhaps with a choking feeling? Some people feel in their mind that they are going crazy when this happens, but the feeling is so intense that they may have wondered if they needed emergency care. Then the feeling passes, and they go on with their life.

Similar to generalized anxiety, there may be other discomforts that accompany the racing heartbeat and choking feeling. They include feeling detached from your body as well as feelings of "shakiness," nausea, and dizziness. A combination of feelings like this would also be cause to get a professional mental health follow-up. Nonprescription and maybe even prescription medication can cause symptoms that feel like the ones I have described, but those symptoms are really just due to the effect of the drugs—not anxiety. Anxiety will not kill you, but it can severely undermine PF. We will talk more in chapter 9 about when to get help.

Living While Black Will Make You Anxious

These days, African American men, women, and children are mistreated and sometimes killed for doing normal things that white people do or could do without a second thought or consequence. In this reality, it is very hard not to worry.

Trayvon Martin walked through a middle-class neighborhood on his way home. He did not walk across a dangerous freeway. He had purchased a bag of Skittles from a nearby store. He did not make it home that night. Instead, he was killed by a neighborhood watchman who had been told to stay in his car and not approach Trayvon. Two years later, Tamir Rice was twelve years old when he played in a park for the last time. He was shot by police who indicated that he had been told to drop his "weapon." How many times did you watch the video or listen to Diamond Reynolds as she kept her composure while pleading with the police officer, who shot her boyfriend, to tell her that her boyfriend wasn't dead? My own heart broke even more for her daughter who sat still in the back of the car. You never heard the child scream or cry. At some point, she told her mother, "It's okay. I'm right here with you." These stories go on and on because police kill Black people on 300 out of 365 days each year.[16]

There is a sickness in our society that has given you *plenty* of reason to worry. When the story of Trayvon's death unfolded in the television news coverage, you may have felt keyed up, tense, and angry. As time passed, you may become emotionally numb to police violence, but when you were subjected one year later to the trial for Trayvon's 2012 murder, you relived much of the same intense emotions. Clinically, experts say that your emotional response should be in proportion to the stressful situation. I acknowledge that it isn't so straightforward and not very easy to explain, but while the threats in our society that make you worry are real, there are ways to cope that can be helpful:

- Be intentional about how you think about and manage reactions to racial injustice. Take time to write your thoughts and feelings in a journal. Otherwise, the thoughts replay in your mind and intensify your worry.

- Even if you do not have the opportunity to journal, ask yourself, "What about all of this is most upsetting to me?" Maybe your heart hurts for the murdered child's mother. Perhaps you wonder if things will ever get better.

- If it is in the news, you may have to begin by limiting your exposure to social media, where the outrageous scene plays over and over. Though it is good to be informed, think about what is in your control and how exposure to senseless violence undercuts your PF.

- Get active. Join or start an advocacy group that challenges the use of force in policing or join a larger group, such as Moms Demand Action for Gun Sense in America. This was one step taken by Lucy McBath, the mother of Jordan Davis, who was killed because he was enjoying loud music with his friends. Mrs. McBath is now a United States Congresswoman.

The thing about anxiety is that the cause of the actual anxiety does not matter. What matters is what you do in response to your fear and how you manage your worry. The cause of your anxiety could be frustration about never-ending disrespect from a supervisee, agitation about a potential bully at your daughter's school, or the police response to a shooting in the next town over, but first assess your mind-set about the situation. If you can join an advocacy group, pushing in the same direction with like-minded others will be more helpful than re-exposing yourself to the TV drama from your kitchen table.

The Ways Anxiety Runs On and On in Your Head

Because there are multiple types of anxiety, it can be difficult to diagnose, but recognizing anxiety for what it is will be key to getting relief. I describe here symptoms and signs of anxiety not to suggest that you diagnose yourself, which is not recommended. Instead, my goal is to point out some key features of various anxiety problems. I do not want to create a manual for self-diagnosis but to instead give you some language that you might use to follow up on your concern because anxiety shows up in many different ways, and are described in the *Diagnostic and Statistical Manual of Mental Disorders* that mental health professionals use to determine when a problem has emerged.[17] If you or a loved one is experiencing any of these challenges, psychological fortitude will be compromised. There is no way around it. With some understanding and an intentional plan to consult with a professional, you can achieve higher fortitude than you have had for as long as you can remember.

Rumination

When your boyfriend makes plans without you on the anniversary of your first date and you replay over and over why he would do such a thing, that is rumination. You are not going to come up with the answer to his poor planning on your own. Replaying that exasperating situation keeps you from communicating effectively and can worsen your mood. Rather than addressing the true source of the problem, you end up paralyzed with inaction and no solution. If you ruminate in your head about the situation, this is not helpful and only serves to escalate anxiety and especially depression. Can you recall a single occasion in which you felt better after you ruminated over the time that you were mistreated? Rumination is not a disorder, but a feature of both anxiety and depression. Rumination is the negative thoughts in your head that replay like a vinyl record that skips repetitively due to a scratch. Those scratched records would play the same annoying pop and skip until someone picked the "needle" up and moved it beyond the scratch. If you do not move the needle along, you end up in a perpetual state of anger and frustration.

Social Phobia

If you avoid people or are paralyzed with fear by the very thought of talking to a room full of strangers, this could be considered a type of anxiety disorder that is known as social phobia. If avoidance of people goes on for six months or more and keeps you from making new friends or meeting a potential romantic partner (which you've been praying for!), that is problematic. You may have been convinced that something is wrong with you or that you are an extreme introvert. You can tolerate your family on holidays and do okay at work, where you are pretty isolated from people. However, if you were ever asked to talk to a group of people about your important work, you would be paralyzed with fear. The problem isn't you. The problem is your thoughts. You are not your thoughts. The thoughts say that people are judging you and that you will do something embarrassing. The thoughts say that as long as you can avoid such situations, you will be better off. Unfortunately, you are also unable to make friends and feel terribly isolated. You can see a professional who is skilled in alleviating these anxieties. Cognitive behavioral therapists have been addressing these types of challenges for years.

Agoraphobia

You may have a cousin who is about your age but stuck at home on disability. No one knows exactly what is wrong with her, but over the years, she became increasingly afraid of driving. At one point, she was afraid to leave her home. She might be agoraphobic. Agoraphobia is also treatable, but you can imagine the difficulty when you know that treatment requires that your cousin will have to face her fear. Over the years, you and other family members gave up on trying to convince her to drive, though everyone got tired of chauffeuring her around. Since she was always "different," everyone decided to leave her be. She always seemed highly uncomfortable in crowds and public places. As a teenager, she wouldn't even go to the movies with you.

Specific Fears

People who have serious fears of very specific things, such as snakes, bridges, airplanes, and so on, are said to have "phobias." This is different from more generalized anxiety, where you have a lot of worry about many different types of things. There is some research that suggests that Black people have higher rates of phobias than do white people. Perhaps these phobias coincide with pervasive trauma generation after generation. I do not know of any research that speaks to why racial differences might occur. This is one of those topics that would be well served to have more researchers who are invested in understanding PF challenges from an African American perspective. I know that I have a certain "insect" fear that I am not going to write about here because I do not want to see the word on the page. As a point of distinction, my fear does not keep me from going camping in wooded areas with my favorite Cub Scout. I am cautious, but not so much that I cannot support my son. Fears become problematic when they keep you from doing the things that you want or need to do. If you do not know if you have a serious fear or phobia, but you have a fear that impacts your life in ways that you prefer not to be impacted, you can see a professional who can diagnose your concern.

Obsessive-Compulsive behavior (OCD)

This is no longer considered a type of anxiety as it once was, but the *evidence-based* treatment is similar to what we use for people with anxiety disorders. OCD is also a concern for which we need more researchers who are invested in Black children and adults to better understand the very complex challenges that can lead to OCD. The main feature of OCD is uncomfortable, inappropriate, or unwanted thoughts that will not go away. The person who has the thoughts or urges may do something that they think will help address the thoughts or help them feel better or be less anxious or upset. But they gain only temporary relief. Imagine that you are upset by your hands getting dirty. You have already washed them three times vigorously with soap in the last two minutes, but you wash them again because you are unconvinced that your hands are clean. You feel that if you wash them one more time, you will feel better, but you are upset again within a few minutes.

Preliminary research suggests that African Americans suffer more than white people from fears of "contamination" or worries about germs and getting sick. If you are someone who fears germs, you will do whatever is necessary to feel clean and manage your germ-related anxiety.

While some manage anxiety with obsessive cleaning, others manage anxiety with hoarding behavior. You may be someone who has accumulated so much stuff that you cannot move around in your own home. Each new thing that you add to your "collection" gives you joy. It would be upsetting to think about ridding yourself of any of your stuff. You have brothers and other family members who express concern or give you a hard time about all of your stuff, but you ignore them all. You are likely engaging in hoarding. If so, it is indicative of your best approach to managing anxiety.

OCD includes hoarding, being overly concerned that things are symmetrical, religious obsessions, and also sexual obsessions that occur only in the mind. Each of these can be disruptive for a person's life. Your grandmother may have been religious and prayed frequently all of her life, but she would not be considered to have obsessions unless she first *feared* committing a sin and then had to *make up* for the sin. Obsessive thoughts are highly upsetting. The person who experiences the thoughts believes that they are dangerous. If your grandma has thoughts that are obsessive in nature, she would do something like pray for a specific number of times to atone or make up for her feared sin. Other types of obsessions can be sexual in nature and include inappropriate thoughts about a family member. To neutralize the thought, the troubled young woman might do mental counting. The "compulsive" counting and praying behavior can be disruptive, but more importantly, those behaviors can be treated by a professional who uses evidence-based therapies for obsessions and compulsive behavior.

Hair-Pulling and Skin-Picking

When I was a child, one of my little cousins pulled her hair. She would wrap it around her little finger and pull so often that she had bald spots in her hair. Because she was very little, her hair pulling was presumably no different than sucking her thumb. However, if your teenage daughter pulls her hair out, it could be something that needs your attention. I do not know how common these problems are, but I mention them because (1) they are problems that are seen as normal in our communities though they are not, and (2) they are treatable. People who pick at their skin typically think they are making it better but are instead making it worse. Your friend who picks at her nail cuticles until they bleed? She cannot seem to stop because she can't. In addition to being physically painful, it can be isolating as she avoids embarrassing situations where people can see her hands. Biting the nails and also pulling on skin on other parts of the body—also not good.

Post-Traumatic Stress Disorder (PTSD)

Like OCD, PTSD is treated similarly to the evidence-based therapy approach used for anxiety. This includes confronting the feelings or numbness and avoidance linked to the trauma. Compared to people from other racial and ethnic groups, African Americans are believed to suffer disproportionately more from PTSD symptoms, such as nightmares, irritation, and thoughts about a trauma that won't go away. Because of the unacknowledged trauma in our communities, we have to spend some time here just to scratch the surface of this painful problem for our community.

When people think of PTSD, they typically think of war veterans. However, the trauma that can cause PTSD can happen to anyone. An experience is considered "traumatic" if you or someone that you are close to is in a violent situation in which someone dies, there is a threat of death, or other violence. If you were raped or witnessed the death or near death of someone you care about, you could be traumatized. If you did not personally witness a violent situation, you could still be at risk if you learn of some violence toward someone you care about. Experts cannot predict who will develop PTSD symptoms following a trauma. It is best to assume that anyone could develop a traumatic stress response.

As much as you want to be helpful, telling your line sister "not to think about it" does not eliminate her upsetting thoughts about her rape. To you, she may seem excessively "jumpy" and try to avoid situations that remind her of the traumatic event. She may feel like she is not herself anymore. The things that she avoids may make no sense to you, but they make complete sense to her. The same fireworks that you enjoy on the Fourth of July may escalate war-related fears among veterans or among those who have experienced gun violence. If you experienced a life-changing trauma, you may have nightmares or flashbacks for months or years if left untreated.

Sadly, Black women and girls are more likely than other women and girls to be victims of sexual violence and domestic violence. Too often Black girls are considered "fast" for having sexual relations with men who are somehow excused. It is a troubling mark on a community that defends the perpetrators. Child victims do not "outgrow" trauma. If unaddressed with a professional, these victims are affected for the remainder of their lives.

If you watched *Surviving R. Kelly*, you were no doubt sickened by the stories and saddened by the women's pain. No one could go through what the girls and women in the documentary described and be unaffected. Unfortunately, the predatory behavior on Black girls and women persists well beyond Robert Kelly's sphere. If you tell your young daughter to let you know if anyone ever touches her, but you tell her that she must have "misunderstood," you are contributing to the problem. To break the cycles, be vigilant and listen to your daughter (*and* your son), even if no one listened to you.

TRAUMA SYMPTOMS COULD DELAY

If you are a trauma survivor who begins to experience tightness in your chest and unexplained sweatiness weeks after a traumatic experience, that is not surprising. Do not ever give yourself a hard time for not being over the tragic death of someone important or having gone through a traumatic situation. A student recently told me that an administrator at the university expressed surprise that he was still dealing with the death of his sister from a car accident just over a year ago. The student was doing his best to move on but was having problems in classes. The anniversary of his sister's death, his sister's birthday, other important occasions, and a seemingly random song on the radio will always be reminders of his sister. If someone close to you has died or if you have experienced trauma, you can try to squash your upset, but it will keep coming back until you deal with it. Find someone whom you can work with so you can work through PTSD symptoms.

Research shows that trauma symptoms following a hurricane disaster in Florida did not show up for Black and Hispanic people for months. As you know, there were many poor and even not-so-poor Black and brown people who lost everything during hurricanes Katrina and Harvey. Months and years later, they tell themselves that they should be over it. Researchers have reported specific findings from hurricane-related disasters, but I suspect that the same symptom delay could occur regardless of the traumatic experience.[18]

EXCESSIVE MEDIA CONSUMPTION DOES NOT HELP

Media seems to contribute to vicarious trauma. Recently, I had a conversation with a woman from church. She described a local murder that had been repeatedly broadcasted on the news. When I asked how she has been feeling about the endless murders, I could not help but notice that she tensed up before she responded to my question. She disclosed that she has been very upset about how things are going in our society. I asked if she could turn off the television, but she was adamant that she needed to keep up with everything so she knew what was going on "out there." I suggested that while she might feel that it is important to be aware of local events, her awareness comes with consequences. She agreed. When I saw her again several weeks later, she still hadn't decreased her exposure to the news. In her mind perhaps, the need to know outweighed the angst that it was visibly causing her.

There is some research that shows that African Americans have been experiencing trauma-related anxiety in response to the chronic media exposure to violent deaths of African Americans. You may be wondering how someone who is not directly or even indirectly affected by violence would have heightened anxiety. I suspect that in any one of these unarmed shooting incidents, you can imagine someone close to you who could be targeted. Each time you hear of another unnecessary murder of an unarmed person, you feel anger and a sense of helplessness. You may internalize the message that people like you do not matter. You may be saddened or enraged. In any case, these are all reactions to an awful and pervasive problem in our society—a problem that has meaningful psychological consequences. Research shows that Black people report poorer emotional health for one to two months following the police shooting of an unarmed Black person.[19]

Untreated PTSD is a serious problem. Without professional help, saying that you should be over it "by now" does not make it true no matter how much you desperately want to move on. I advise that if someone you know has gone through something unimaginable and life-changing, they cannot expect to go on with life as if the life-changing event never occurred.

Sleep Paralysis

The last anxiety-related problem that I want to mention is sleep paralysis. It is one that is understudied in general but seems to be more common in Black people compared to white people. Sleep paralysis is just as it sounds and occurs just as you are falling asleep or just waking up. It is not a problem per se but can be a bit freaky because you are awake but inexplicably unable to physically move. It is a temporary experience that lasts for a few minutes or less. Experts do not know a lot about sleep paralysis but have said that it can be caused by stress and trauma.

Unfortunately, the best way to treat serious types of anxiety involves doing the very thing that the person most fears. More serious types of anxiety cannot be solved without tackling the problem head-on. I would venture to say that it cannot be solved by prayer alone unless prayer involves asking for guidance on which professional to schedule an appointment with. If your anxiety is so bad that it interferes with your work, school, or (nonexistent) social life, then you may need medication. Like therapy, medication does not always work the first time out. It can require constant communication with the psychiatrist. While you might trust your primary care physician, a prescription from her may not be as useful as a prescription from a psychiatrist, who is trained in what we call *psychotropic* medication. We will talk more about how treatment works in chapter 10, but I mention it here to highlight that these challenges are treatable, and it is actually important that you get some help if you are to live the life that you were put on Earth to live.

The Struggle Can Be Inherited

I am often asked, "Does mental illness run in families?" When you ask this question of me, I hear the disguised but noticeable fear in your voice. It sounds like an intellectual question, but the fear is heavy when you are thinking about your fourteen-year-old daughter or son.

Say your son has never given you or your husband (his stepdad) any trouble and rarely got into trouble in school. He was an only child who has always been one of the smartest in his class. Whereas, you got into trouble for talking too much in school, your son only talks when necessary. His teachers have always seen him as a good student. When he was younger, he tolerated other children, but you noticed that he stayed to himself more and more as he got older. When you had another baby five years ago, your son's level of detachment became particularly noticeable. In the last few months, you have found that he gets very impatient with his little brother and sometimes spends hours and hours alone in his room. When you ask him to join the family, he is present, but still not connected. It just feels odd. Sometimes he reminds you of his (biological) father who got very depressed sometimes, though not when he is taking his "bipolar medication." It scares you to think that your child could have a serious problem.

The short answer to your fearful question is, "Yes, psychological problems can run in families." Serious problems like schizophrenia, where the affected person has lost touch with reality, and bipolar disorder, when the person has erratic mood swings, are more likely to be inherited than other less severe types of problems (like phobias).

When psychologists and other mental health professionals ask about family history and discover that someone in the family suffers from mental or emotional health challenges, they tend not to be surprised. Obviously, not everyone whose family has members with mental health problems will inherit the same types of disorders. Sometimes what people inherit is a *vulnerability* or a predisposition that is triggered by a stressful situation. They have a low tolerance for stress. In the example, your son may have challenges because of a biological predisposition that was triggered, or he may have learned to retreat to his room because of what he saw when his grandfather managed stress with explosive anger. When we say that problems run in families, we are more likely to see psychological problems in individuals when other family members (living or deceased) have such challenges.

Shifting an Anxious Perspective Toward Positive Change

As humans, we find ways to deal with life's adversities the best way that we can. You may have been in a car accident, and as a result, you prefer not to drive. You may actually be scared to drive but not tell anyone of your fear. You just refuse to drive. Alternatively, you can begin to shift your perspective in these ways:

- First, recognize your challenge for what it is: a challenge to be overcome. Unless you have a hidden superpower, you cannot change the things that happened in the past.

- You can decide to change today, or you can decide not to change at all. Either way, you are making a decision.

- If you tell yourself that your fear of something, like driving, signifies that you are "crazy," then you have put undue pressure on yourself. This pressure will make your situation harder to get out from under. Being crazy is yet another hurdle that you have to overcome—as if you do not have enough to do already.

- If you think of the problem as something that is "not helpful," you put yourself on the path to creating solutions that are more likely attainable.

When Depression Sneaks In

Imagine an African American mother who works full time and is very active in her community. At work, she is a supervisor who is responsible for multiple employees (and their difficult personalities). She is a good-hearted person who takes it all in stride. At home, she cooks meals, keeps the house clean, and makes sure that her children do their homework. She also makes sure that they get to their numerous extracurricular activities throughout the academic year, including sports on Saturdays. She is in church every Sunday and sometimes volunteers with one of the ministries. In the community, she holds office in two civic organizations.

As you might imagine, she is tired, chronically stressed, and sleep-deprived, but she lies awake at night for hours because she cannot fall asleep. She oftentimes has problems concentrating at work and no longer knows what gives her joy. When she stops to think, she feels tearful and sometimes wants to run away from it all. She could be depressed. She could also be managing a tremendous amount of anxiety. Though she does an impressive job of keeping everything together for appearances, the effort in doing so only adds to her stress. Her first step is to talk to someone who can diagnose the problem.

Has it been so long that you got joy out of life that you don't even remember what you enjoy? In general, depression is low mood or disinterest in things that were interesting at one time, but it does not end there. Based on our usual definitions, you might be sad and irritable and also sleep ten-hour days, overeat, and have thoughts of suicide. Someone you know could sleep relatively little, lose eighteen pounds in two months, and never consider suicide, but feel on the inside that life is worthless.

Because life just happens to all of us, if you have a few hours or a couple of days when these types of feelings or experiences happen, you would not meet the threshold for depression. However, if it goes on for weeks or months or years, it could be depression. Notice that I say it "could" be depression. You may want to get a thorough physical exam that includes a thyroid check to rule out health problems. Your thyroid is a gland that controls how your body metabolizes food that you eat. When your thyroid underperforms, you may feel tired and depressed with generally low energy and prefer to sleep all the time. These are thyroid problems that can cause or mimic depression.

Your Depression Is Not Becky's Depression

What inspired me to earn a PhD is the assumption in mainstream psychology that Black people's depression looks the same as that of white people. Many African Americans (or at least the ones who identify as African American) assume that Black people do things differently, see things differently, feel things differently, and even say things differently than do white people. For anyone to assume that psychology is the same regardless of race is to operate from a place of privilege. Those who "do not see race" presume that there is no reality that exists outside of their own. My work is about bringing attention to our mental health realities. Depression can look different because not everyone has the same symptoms, even within racial or ethnic groups, but also because of our cultural lenses.

I like the labels that Dr. F. M. Baker introduced in 2001 to describe the experience of depression.[20] He described the "detached long-sufferer" who proclaims that faith in God is the answer to all and the "John Henry Doer" whose health is compromised by overworking but nevertheless persists in overworking. Both are labels to which I can relate for depressed African Americans.

The data-supported research suggests that though a Black person and a white person might seem to have the same level of depression symptoms, the Black person will not acknowledge thoughts of suicide and may be more likely to acknowledge other depression symptoms (e.g., sleep problems). Even still, they may also get out of bed and go to work every day and not miss a day for forty years. They may not "feel" depressed, but that does not mean that the depression is not there. It only means that the depression profile is different and thus more likely to fly under the radar. Unfortunately, your physician may not be familiar with the preliminary research that describes potential depression profiles for Black people. Though I believe there to be value in the profiles, much more research is needed to solidify them.

Understanding Confusing Statistics

If you have ever taken it upon yourself to read about depression statistics or if you have ever been in an audience where someone was talking about depression statistics, you may have heard some conflicting information. On the one hand, Black people are more likely than white people to report or say that they have symptoms of depression. At the same time, Black people are less likely to meet the criteria for a depression diagnosis.

How can both be true? For you to meet criteria for a depression diagnosis, you have to endorse certain symptoms. If you do not endorse those symptoms, the interviewer does not "check the box" for depression. In the end, you can endorse a number of symptoms and to a high degree, but if you do not endorse the *right* symptoms, then you do not meet the criteria no matter how many of the other symptoms were checked or for how long they have been experienced.

Whether or not we have more or less depression is less important than the fact that by the time we seek help, our symptoms tend to be unnecessarily debilitating; compared to white women and men, our symptoms tend to be more severe and less amenable to intervention because we wait so long to get help. We must stop waiting until things are so bad off that they are irreversible.

Revisiting Diabetes and Depression

I mentioned in chapter 3 that serious health conditions, like diabetes, are further complicated by poor psychological fortitude. A depressed person may experience low mood or disinterest in life. They may be irritable, sleep excessively, have a tendency to overeat, and hide thoughts of taking their life. Imagine having both symptoms of depression and type 2 diabetes to manage. The consequences of mismanaging them, however, are that you lose your sight, end up with an amputated limb, or worse. It may be hard to think about health together with psychological fortitude, but what if the health problems that run in the family could be interrupted if the PF problems were addressed?

When I talk to people about this, everyone agrees that it makes sense that people with health problems are prone to depression. What you may not know is that people who are diagnosed with diabetes are *twice* as likely as those not diagnosed with diabetes to be depressed. Type 2 diabetes is a leading cause of death among African Americans. Since there isn't a mental health professional set up adjacent to most endocrinologist offices in the United States, you will have to be patient yet proactive on behalf of yourself and loved ones.

Consider what people diagnosed with diabetes are expected to be able to do while being depressed. It seems unreasonable that you would expect your uncle to exercise regularly, avoid his favorite pound cake, and remember medication each day. Keep in mind that you may have a difficult time exercising and eating healthy even without serious PF limitations. Nevertheless, this is what is expected of people who manage diabetes. I have not investigated depression and other serious health concerns, but I have no doubt that you can apply the depression to any condition that requires management.

Struggles in Childhood Affect How Your Body Copes Now

If you have persistently low psychological fortitude, I suspect that you have had a profoundly troubling life challenge—a challenge that you did not have the resources at the time to manage. This is why abuse and neglect that happen in childhood have so much impact for the remainder of our lives. Your childhood was the most vulnerable stage of your life because you did not have the maturity to understand what was happening to and around you. So it is important for you to get your PF up so you can be watchful of your children and help them deal with adversity.

According to experts, "childhood adversity" compromises how the body responds to stress. If not neutralized by a supportive environment, childhood adversity can lead to alcoholism, heart disease, anxiety, depression, and all kinds of other problems in adulthood. If you were abused or neglected as a child, you are at risk for a poorer quality of life than those who experienced no adversity, though you may not think of yourself as "at risk." Bad things can happen throughout life, but childhood is vulnerable even if you were "mature for your age." Again, to stop damaging cycles, be vigilant in protecting your loved ones.

Stress Is Not Just in Your Head, It Harms Your Whole Being

You may have reached that stage of life wherein your physician is recommending extra tests because you have complained of chest pain or some other troublesome ache. Once the tests are completed and the physician rules out everything that you could be tested for, he says, "Have you been under a lot of stress?"

You respond with a chuckle. What you really want to say is, "You're kidding, right? Don't I look like I've been under a lot of stress? What do you mean by 'stress'?" The last thought is the funniest because you wonder when the time was that you were not under a lot of stress.

When the doctor asks about stress, it seems to be a throw away category—if there is no physical cause, it must be in your head. But the stress question is a very real one. Your physician is not suggesting that you are crazy. Instead, he is suggesting that you may want to take inventory of the stressors in your life and how you are managing them. When you do not have what you need to appropriately manage your stress, your body does what it can to manage the stress "threats" for you, which hurts your overall physical health.

Be Alert to Misdiagnosis

While anxiety and depression are the most commonly occurring threats to PF, they are not the most common conditions people think about when they think of "mental illness." Most people are thinking about more severe conditions, like schizophrenia, whereby the individual has lost touch with reality. A person with schizophrenia may hear voices or see things that are not there. They can be excessively paranoid. These types of problems are specifically referred to as "psychosis." Psychosis can be a symptom of severe depression though not often. Again, talking to an expert can help.

One roadblock in the process of gaining information about your PF is misdiagnosis. There are studies that show that you, as a Black person, are more likely to be misdiagnosed than your white peer. Preliminary studies suggest that because of differences in how our symptoms show up, mental health professionals are less equipped to identify our anxiety and depression. The problem with misdiagnosis is that certain problems (such as bipolar disorder) can be treated more efficiently and effectively, and other problems (such as schizophrenia) have a poorer prognosis.

There has been some research that showed that Black people are generally more likely to be diagnosed with schizophrenia than with bipolar disorder, a type of depression. Some people know bipolar disorder as manic depression because the individual seems to cycle from very high mood to very low mood. They may seem crazy and erratic, but it is not the same as behavior that we see for someone who suffers from schizophrenia. Bipolar disorder is treated with medication, and the individual can usually live a full and productive life. People who have severe schizophrenia will often require more assistance, as they are unable to take care of themselves.

I recall a client case that occurred when I was in my doctoral training program. As background, when psychologists do not know what the diagnosis is, but there is preliminary information, we first generate possible diagnoses to "rule out." In this example, a fellow doctoral student indicated that he needed to rule out schizophrenia for an African American male client. When I asked my classmate why he suggested schizophrenia, he referred to the manner in which the gentleman responded to the routine series of questions. He observed that the man was describing "strange experiences" and seemingly paranoid thoughts that people are out to get him or perhaps seeing things that other people do not see. I had overheard this client in the waiting room over a period of time as I worked in an office nearby. The cultural divide that led the classmate to suggest schizophrenia was clear to me.

Unfortunately, observations like this can happen when there is limited guidance for how to interpret Black folks' behavior and beliefs. The field of psychology may not be able to anticipate the ways in which psychological symptoms show up differently for Black adults compared to white adults. By no fault of our own, Black people can seem more paranoid and crazier than people from other racial groups. This paranoia can factor into misdiagnosis because we are perceived as being out of touch with reality. I look forward to the day when cultural competence is the enforced rule and not the exception. Until that day comes, you will need to be proactive in getting the assistance that you need for yourself and for your family.

You Deserve More Than Anxiety and Depression as Your Norm

You probably know someone who has struggled with social phobia, PTSD, or depression for their entire life. This is what we will do and what others will enable us to do. Our suffering feels like our norm. I get it. Anxiety and depression are serious, but often hidden problems because you may not know the symptoms to look for. But now you have more information.

You probably knew that you have a part of your life that you have to "deal with" and feel you have no choice but to do just that. You suck it up and try to live life. You may even think that this is what it means to have psychological fortitude, but this is where I would have to stop you. If you are constantly managing nagging or intrusive thoughts, have a hard time getting out of bed most days, or avoid social situations because you fear that you will do something to embarrass yourself, you are not living life. Your PF is at fifty (out of one hundred) at best. If at the end of the day, it feels like a hamster-wheel existence, it is. You may be waiting for something magical to happen, but magical thinking will not solve the problem.

I know it is especially hard to try to get help when you are overwhelmed, your PF is low, and it already takes everything in you to put one foot in front of the other. To add to this, you simply do not have time to take to get help for yourself when you are also responsible for others.

If too many mental health providers are unsuited to address your concerns, there would seem to be no point in trying. I understand how you could come to this conclusion, but I respectfully disagree. We will talk in chapter 9 about the value of seeking help and not waiting until you are in crisis and in chapter 10 about how to interact with potential providers so they can help you.

Control Your Psychological Fortitude

There are some things that are out of your control, but there are a number of things that are in your control. Racism is out of your control, but how you deal with racism is in your control. Having a family history of high blood pressure is out of your control, but finding out whether the dizziness that you experience on stressful afternoons is due to heart disease or panic symptoms is in your control. If you are healthy and have no serious physical health challenges to manage, you may be ahead of the game for now. However, when either anxiety or depression goes untreated, it undermines quality of life. Anxiety or depression also undermines various aspects of physical health, but especially your ability to maintain or regain health. If you get to a stage of life whereby you have to manage health challenges, know that it is difficult to manage health without high PF.

Did you ever cross your eyes as a kid until your mother told you that your eyes would get stuck like that if you kept it up? I may have been the most naïve child on the planet, but I stopped right away. I did not need to be crossing my eyes for no good reason, and it was no problem to stop. Since your PF is *in* your control, I advise that you practice maximizing it to the best of your ability before it gets stuck. Part 2 of this book is intended to show you how, but let's tackle a couple more elephants before we get there.

CHAPTER 5

Racism Is Bad for You

As a Black woman, I know the balancing act that goes along with having a Black identity—taking care of everyone else and putting the effort into being "put together" despite being invisible. My parents informed me early on that I would have to work twice as hard to get half as far. The reference for the "twice" and "half" were white people. I understood this as my reality and not anything to be challenged. Somewhere along the path to becoming a psychology professor, I developed language that would help me label what people of African descent manage daily.

At times, Blackness is like wearing an invisible veil while navigating through life. You can see through the veil, but your vision is distorted. Interactions with others at work and school remind you that you don't "belong." You value the spaces where you can exist free of this "otherness." It is an annoying hindrance that you have dealt with because it is just part of life. White people do not wear a veil like the one that you wear. They do not see your veil. This veil is made up mostly of race-based discrimination, also known as racism.

You have likely experienced racism at many points in your life. You know what it is when you see it. It is important for you to have a more sophisticated understanding of how racism can operate in your life. Racism is a system that maintains itself. It impacts your health and undermines your PF and the PF of those around you. You need to know this because, sadly, racism is not going anywhere. The veil maintains itself, and it also maintains the resultant inequality that you see in well-being, physical health, education, housing, income, and the (in)justice system—all things that directly or indirectly undermine psychological fortitude.

Let's Get Clear About Research

To share with you the most informed and up-to-date perspective on racism and well-being, I will soon talk about research studies and findings. But first I want to point out the racism within research findings themselves. Yes, it's true that, because the system maintains itself, the ways in which research sheds light (or not) on the status of Black psychological fortitude often puts Black reality on the back burner or on no burner at all. Typically, studies occur when someone has observed a problem that requires a solution or at least some insight. The people who are most qualified to generate hypotheses that make sense for the Black community are those who have intimate knowledge of the inner workings of the community's culture.

Because the culture is so diverse, this task is not to be taken lightly. If people of African descent are not involved in generating the hypothesis or question that forms the basis of research, the study could be ill-informed from the outset. It is the same as when a major department store puts a racist slogan on a Black model.[21] You know there was no conscious Black "representation" in the room when that idiotic selection was made. As an example from my research, we can speculate or hypothesize that the loss of a job increases suicide risk (because of the significant loss of identity). But if someone has an identity that is strongly rooted in being Black or African, the loss of a job may not be as meaningful. Other things are more important. That is not to say that losing one's job is not stressful. Identity is, however, an important factor in how the job loss is experienced—an experience that varies by culture. We have to be involved in psychology research to inform the work that matters for us.

Next, consider the method that is used to test the hypothesis. One of the biggest criticisms of mainstream research has been the unethical and often abusive manner in which Black folks are unwitting participants in research. There have been numerous atrocities committed against Black people in the service of science. These are a few that come to mind:

- You are likely familiar with the Tuskegee syphilis experiment in which syphilis treatment was intentionally withheld from Black men who had been diagnosed with the disease.

- J. Marion Sims, the so-called father of modern gynecological surgery, performed surgeries on enslaved Black women in the nineteenth century with no anesthesia. Harriet Washington details this atrocity and countless others in her book *Medical Apartheid*.[22] It is not an easy read, but I recommend this text because it is part of our historical record of which we are mostly unaware.

- The Maafa or African Holocaust and the abuses that Black people suffered are part of our narrative too. Even when not enslaved, Black people were subjected to "science" at its worst.

- In more benign but still problematic contemporary times, some white researchers go to Black communities to collect data that advances careers, but that does very little, if anything, to improve those communities.

As a result and given the historical context, Black people tend to be understandably reticent to participate in research. Unfortunately, this reticence also applies to those of us who are invested in advancing the community. I understand that it can be hard to separate the good guys from the bad guys.

Mathematical processes determine whether the findings are meaningful and significant. While this may seem a good idea because math is presumably objective, the data that goes into the study, the method, and related factors impact the study results. If the formulation of the problem, the data, and the method are faulty, then there is only so much that the math can tell us.

Health disparities persist in part because health researchers fail to consider our true problems that are often impacted by systemic racism, individual choice, community values, and access to care—all of which are easy to ignore. Consider that African Americans are more likely to be affected by asthma than European Americans. There are treatments available for asthma, but we still have a higher prevalence. If there is something about asthma that makes African Americans more vulnerable, then intervention should address the unique realities that African Americans experience.

I could say so much more about the systems that impact research that would otherwise be useful to us. Suffice it to say that we need more research that is conducted by those who understand and are invested in the community from *within*. We also need to include more research that is based on interviews and focus-group conversations about day-to-day experiences and to better understand the complex realities of Black people in the United States and around the world.

Throughout this book, I acknowledge when research is preliminary or less definitive and needs more work. Assume that if I mention a study and especially how the study was carried out or how many times it was carried out, the findings are as good as they come.

Racism, in All Its Forms, Is Bad for Mental Health

Scientists can say with confidence that racism is bad for Black mental health. This is an area where numerous studies converge on this one conclusion. Multiple experts using different approaches to studying racism-related problems have determined that racial discrimination is psychologically and physically harmful to Black people. This may seem obvious, but even those of us who are well versed in the research likely fail to fully grasp the depth of these findings.

Interestingly, white people have reported that they experience racial discrimination. But this self-reported experience is not as compelling as the data that shows that for Black people, dysregulation in the bodily response to stress via high blood pressure is in part attributed to racism. In a study of Black women in Detroit, researchers collected data for 343 women over the course of five years.[23] These types of data gathered over time (rather than the more common approach of getting data at a "snapshot" in time) are impressive because the researchers can account for numerous potential causes for the outcome that they hope to predict. In this study, they found that more discrimination was associated with poorer health and more depression. This was true even after considering the age, income level, and education of the study participants. Typically, older people and those with less formal education and fewer resources tend to have poorer physical health, but that simply did not matter in the Detroit study. One preliminary study found that atherosclerosis, which is typically associated with smoking and high cholesterol, was linked to discrimination experiences among African American women. Again, the researchers controlled for other factors that commonly lead to atherosclerosis. Racism was bad, and neither age nor social status mattered.

I could reference more and more studies, but the findings are largely the same: racism is bad for your health. You may be skeptical of "research" because the narratives sometimes change. I recall years ago when researchers said that eggs were bad because they were high in cholesterol, but then more recent studies indicated that they were not. I do not expect to see such a change that racism does not have adverse consequences. Instead, researchers might do a better job of figuring out what mitigates the effects of racism and who might be more resilient.

In my research, I found that experiences of racism were associated with thoughts of suicide for African American adults due to depression, though not for those African Americans who reported having a strong religious connection.[24] We will talk much more about the importance of a religious or spiritual connection in chapter 8. The point here is that racism is physically and emotionally taxing and corrosive for PF. Some people are less vulnerable, but the research on resiliency is limited.

The Experience of Racial Microaggressions

You may have heard of a seemingly tiny thing called racial "microaggressions" that can be worse than overt racism. Racial microaggressions are the subtle racial slights that are negative, demeaning, and sometimes hostile. The most common one that I hear personally here is the "you are so articulate" comment. I often encounter this from colleagues and others who express surprise that I speak so well. Because I am brown, the immediate assumption is that I am not capable of communicating as an educated person who educates others. There was one occasion when a student knocked on my office door. At the time, I was sitting at my desk with my name permanently indicated on the door. There was only one desk. After knocking, the student asked me where he could "find" Dr. Walker. On top of that, a white colleague suggested that I was being sensitive if I thought that the student's question was a microaggression.

Microaggressions can be worse than overt racism because with overt racism (like a cross burning on your lawn), you know what happened, but with racial microaggression, we tend to expend time and cognitive energy processing if what we experienced happened in the way that we felt it and if the negative feeling was warranted. This is a useless exercise, but because we operate in a racialized society, we have to find ways to decipher how we "took" some racialized situation. Not surprisingly, racial microaggression has also been linked to poorer emotional well-being.

When We're Avoided or Overlooked

Academics come up with all sorts of clever names that basically boil down to racism and being mistreated based on one's race. John Dovidio at Yale talks about "aversive racism." I was present many years ago when he gave an enlightening talk about how it works. He described an example of how a white military officer makes a decision about who to promote. Because he is uncomfortable with people who are racially different, he avoids those individuals. He is not mean and does not engage in overtly discriminatory behavior, but he also avoids social contact.

This is problematic because when the time comes to make a decision about who to promote, the officer has more familiarity with those he has engaged with informally compared to those he has avoided. Thus, the person he knows better because of time spent together is more likely to be remembered fondly and get the promotion.

No matter what we call it, being subjected to negative stereotypes and mistreatment is a tremendous psychological burden that continuously rests on your shoulders. It is of no surprise that you feel anxious and easily angered. There is sufficient research that shows that racism is not just another stressor that people deal with. For Black people, racism is linked to poorer mental outcomes and emotional stability even when more general life stressors like work stress, relationship stress, and financial stress are taken into consideration.

In a conversation with literary peers, James Baldwin asserted that "to be a Negro in this country and to be relatively conscious is to be in a rage almost all the time."[25] He was right. It will become increasingly important to find ways to navigate this burden. The reality of racism does not mean that anyone who experiences it will always suffer significant consequences. It is a threat to PF, but those who maintain high PF could be protected from negatively racialized encounters.

A Racist System Cannot Fix Itself

As you have seen in several studies that I mentioned, racism can occur regardless of age, education, or income level. Racism is equal opportunity. When experts talk about disparities in health care in our society, they are talking about differences for people based typically on income and race. Black people tend to be overrepresented among the poor, so race and income are often intertwined, but racism is not exclusive to poor Black people. Middle-income Black folks also endure hardships of racism.

Though many thrive in the United States, it also provides a toxic climate for Black people. A large study of Black Caribbean immigrants found that the longer that they were in the United States, the more likely that they were to experience depression and poor overall health.[26] This says something pretty damning about the society in which we live.

Why can't we be great? At the root of racism and racial disparities is the belief that Black people are not fully human and do not deserve access to the same rights as others. Those who hold racist beliefs tend to deny racism. For some, this racism is intentional. For many, it is not intentional, as they are unaware of the ways in which negative stereotypes influence how they interact with Black people or stand by as Black people are being mistreated by others.

Privileged children learn over time that only their perspective matters; they learn this in the same way that I was taught to work twice as hard. They learn to "not see race." If you mention race, then you are perceived as perpetuating a problem—a problem that they refuse to see.

I am not a Freudian psychologist by any stretch of the imagination, but I do think that there is some merit in the idea of "defense mechanisms" that Freud talked about. Think about defense mechanisms as strong but invisible walls in the mind that protect us from uncomfortable, overwhelming, and perhaps threatening feelings. Those walls or defense mechanisms keep information, facts, and events from our active awareness because if we were aware of the information, we would sink into a very dark place. For example, if you have experienced a traumatic event, you may not remember the details because your mind shielded you from them. For some white people to see what Black people deal with in this society would be a traumatic and emotionally devastating experience. So they employ all kinds of defense mechanisms, such as denial and rationalizing (yes, rationalizing is considered a defense mechanism), so as not to even perceive the problems of racism.

Racism Is Hard to Escape

Can you even imagine what it would look like to truly be free, to not have to make any decisions for yourself or your family under the veil of race? I am not sure that I can. The recent rash of African American deaths at the hands of law enforcement officials has a lasting and profound effect on the individual and collective Black psyche, primarily because the kind of injustice resulting from police brutality and state-sanctioned violence is not new. Our community has suffered this kind of treatment for a very long time.

Despite having a PhD and a highly respected occupation, I still receive the clear message that my life is ultimately expendable. Some months after Sandra Bland's very disturbing arrest and suspicious death in Waller County, Texas, I was stopped in my neighborhood by the local police for failure to yield. I live in a large, ethnically diverse, planned community, but as two police officers approached on both sides of my car, I thought about my son and whether or not I would see him again. Though I try not to, I think about that day every time I stop at that intersection.

It would be wonderful to focus on our collective brilliance and not have to navigate racism that is inherent in every system relevant to mankind. It saddens me greatly that, each day, Black children are subject to undue scrutiny and unfair treatment in classrooms where they are supposed to be learning. As a result, our sons and daughters become unwilling participants in disproportionate school suspension statistics for Black preschoolers and elementary-age children. My husband and I both have psychology PhDs, but I doubt we will be able to protect our son from unfair classroom treatment. Even if suspensions are not in a child's future, any classroom behavior that compromises a child's confidence in herself is unacceptable.

The Field of Psychology Is Far Behind Being of Actual Help

The reality is that mental health disciplines have the capacity to improve psychological fortitude for Black people, but it has to be a very intentional process. Instead, institutions are seemingly stacked against the Black community. The discipline of psychology is made better with racial and ethnic diversity, but sincere efforts to address the psychology of a people who have been systematically subjected to inhumane treatment are relatively nonexistent. After all, psychology is the field of study that provided "evidence" that Black people are inferior to white people.[27] In more contemporary times, there are those of us who are dedicated to addressing research and developing culturally informed therapy, but we do so in spite of and not because of the systems that undermine our efforts at just about every turn.

We cannot anticipate that such a system will either dissolve suddenly or operate in a way that is benevolent toward Black people. While there are many white individuals who have worked tirelessly to solve the problem of inequity, the system is rigged. Mental health disciplines are not a part of the solution when they:

- systematically withhold pieces of the mental health puzzle for underserved people

- foster blind spots by demeaning research that addresses unique mental health concerns

- fail to admit ethnically diverse students in the most competitive doctoral programs

- permit "diversity day" in graduate classrooms rather than integrating diversity throughout education and training

Because these are part of the fabric of research and training, the community will have to rely on itself for real change.

Glimmers of Opportunity for a Better Mental Health System

Our society is greatly in need of honest conversation at every level. When mental health providers learn about depression-related misdiagnosis that is more likely to occur for Black relative to white people, they are more attentive to how they engage with Black and African American patients and clients. Over the years, I have been inspired by those doctoral students who use their new insights to promote social justice in psychology.

Depending on the nature of classroom dynamics, students of color are relieved to talk about the lives that they live every day—lives that very few white folks are inclined to discuss. I am that professor who will gladly lead a conversation about race, culture, the difference between the two, how discrimination affects everyday people, why we cannot get along, and so on. When I address topics of racism and racial disparity, white graduate students are often in disbelief (1) about racialized mistreatment and (2) that the insights were well documented but novel to them.

In my multicultural class and in clinical supervision, I tell students that they cannot avoid talking to clients about race if they are seeing a client who is racially or ethnically different from them. We spend a fair amount of time discussing this topic because my advice has oftentimes been contrary to how students in clinical psychology PhD programs are advised. Many faculty members are (unknowingly) uncomfortable talking about race and pass this discomfort on to doctoral students in training. This will not change for the foreseeable future, though the demographics of our society will. What this means for you is that you will have to expend some energy generating your therapist options. Therapists who can talk about race and racism do exist, but you will have to look the way that you do for your hairstylist when you move to a new city. We will talk more in chapter 10 about what to look for in a culturally sensitive therapist and how to make therapy work for you.

I recall a conversation with a white graduate student who was enrolled in my multicultural psychology course years ago. She was an advanced student who was in her second or third year of seeing psychotherapy clients. Without going into detail, the student seemed to understand that her Black female client might feel a certain way about her as a white therapist. They had never discussed this, even though their sessions had been ongoing for maybe a year or more.

On an occasion that seemed appropriate, the therapist asked the client if she thought that she had been mistreated at work because of her race. What the client did next shocked the therapist. The client began to cry. The therapist told me later that their entire dynamic in psychotherapy changed after that day. The client began to make significantly more progress. They had gotten to the root of the problem and were able to develop a more effective strategy for therapy.

Though I provide clinical supervision, I was not supervising this case. It is not unusual for therapists in training to approach me directly because they are working with an African American client and their supervisor is uncomfortable discussing race. Here was a client in psychotherapy for months, doing her best to improve, with the burden of racism on her back but with no discussion of it with her therapist. I assume that the client was getting something out of therapy. That is why she remained, but many do not stay. If your therapy process is raising your PF and helping you meet your goals, that improvement is mission critical. If your therapist seems to struggle when you attempt to introduce your experience as a Black woman, you can let her know you're concerned that she is uncomfortable so she can address it and perhaps get her own consultation outside of therapy.

There are some psychotherapy techniques that have universal success regardless of race. Others are limited in a society that is too often influenced by race. Racism is itself a unique stressor that trained professionals often elude. That does not mean that you have to pretend to not be Black for your white therapist.

Research Can Indirectly Amplify PF

Good research that is developed with you in mind can facilitate high PF. Such research considers your social challenges (like racism) and cultural strengths (like spirituality). Instead, you have to subscribe to pseudoscience and old wives' tales because at least they seem to be culturally informed. Because of a multilayered system of racism and one-size-fits-all mentality, there have been limited advances in understanding and treating mental health problems for African American men, women, and children.

Because many of the people who are considered mental health experts have not had you in mind, there is an assumption that your depression looks like everyone else's depression and the solution to your depression also looks like everyone else's. It is baffling on some level because we tend to acknowledge potential differences in depression for men and women. Men are believed to "stuff" their feelings because they are socialized to "man up" and not show weakness. Women are more likely to try talking through problems. As clinicians, we generate solutions keeping in mind that clients will respond differently due to individual differences and that these differences are sometimes due to one's background. Where we fall short is that the "toolkit" for how to help Black people is stuck in the hot comb phase of emotional health with no Madam C. J. Walker in sight.

Even if you ignore racism, it won't disappear. On the one hand, we know how truly detrimental racism is, but nothing is being done to systematically end it. Closing Starbucks for one day in response to staff racial "insensitivity" will not cure racism and racial bias. The system will not change, and I truly believe that because racism operates as the veil on most days, many African Americans are merely getting by. On a scale of 0 to 100, I would say that getting by looks like 70 PF. The level of PF that is needed to function optimally is 85+, but I wonder how many of us know what that looks like.

Advanced research would help us better understand the insidious nature of discrimination. Preliminary epigenetics research suggests that the effects of racism are passed from one generation to the next. Imagine that! The effects that racism has on your body are passed on to your children. They were passed on to you from your ancestors, who lived under the most devastating conditions. It is no wonder that you're not angrier than you are about the circumstances in which you find yourself.

It is highly likely that your mother and grandmother "made do" with what they had. They may have been amazing at making a way out of no way. They survived in the manner in which they saw others survive. But I would like to see you get to a PF of 95, where racism has very little to no impact on your PF and where sexism has no impact. And where discrimination occurs, but you are inoculated against it and integrated in a community of similarly minded individuals who support you in accessing your true identity—the identity that has not simply survived but thrived. This is the vision that I hope to help you obtain.

Research Validates What We Already Know and Live

More than a decade ago, Dr. Phillip Goff and his colleagues published a study that showed very impressively that white people basically do not see Black people as human.[28] You may have seen this narrative. It is consistent with the study that found medical school students who were less likely in a medical setting to administer pain medication to Black people in a hypothesized scenario.

Of course, there are also more obvious instances of bias whereby Black men and women are presumed dangerous just by living life. It is infuriating and even more so when our own people who are trained in law enforcement and to navigate danger are perpetrators in Black death. In Goff's study, university students presumably did not grow up in an age where popular media provided ingrained racist images that connect Black folks to apes (the study was done before LeBron James's *Vogue* cover). One intriguing outcome in the study was that both white and non-white study participants operated based on racist stereotypes and bias. I was not surprised. Though many are shocked when Black people behave in racist ways toward other Black people, the reality is that Black police officers and others are well versed in the stereotypes that we are aggressive, lazy, and so on. That's why it does not matter if the police officer is Black.

Goff works with Dr. Jennifer Eberhardt, who has received a "genius award" for her research. I think that her research findings should be presented in K–12 schools and in classrooms. Over the years, Dr. Eberhardt has been responsible for very impressive research that shows a lot of what we know already. As an example, police officers are (at best) less respectful to Black people compared to white people. Altogether, the research may feel a bit overwhelming in how consistently it shows what we already know about disparate treatment and racism.

The Delusion at the Core of Mistreatment

Dangerous is the pairing of the delusion that (1) Black people are not human with the belief that (2) white people are (inherently) better than Black people just by nature of being white. In the end, it is all racism, which Dr. Asa Hilliard characterized as a mental disorder.[29]

According to Hilliard, racism would qualify as a mental disorder in part because a person would have to be disconnected from reality to believe that their skin complexion makes them superior to a group of people who do not share that complexion. When you think of someone who experiences such a disconnect, you might imagine someone who also talks to imaginary people on the street, but psychological problems can show up in different ways.

If you think of racism this way, it is beneficial for you to realize that you have been mistreated not because of who you are, but because of something that is wrong with racist people. This could give you some measure of relief, as well as some sense of what you are dealing with. Your constant self-questioning of your own perceptions can end. You may need to sit with this for a while because it is important for you to realize. Despite the persistence of the messages you receive that Black people are the problem, this messaging is fake news.

It's a Universal Experience Among Us

This chapter was not meant to take the wind out of your sails—if anything, I hope to motivate you to collectively look into what we mostly survive day to day. Though the situation is bad, I cannot help but wonder how Black men and women endure with a modicum of sanity in the world that we live in. I do not believe it to be chance.

Some would say that the injustice is not so rampant. If Black people just act "right," they will be fine. However, for every Black person who was not mistreated because of racism, there were likely ten others who were. For those who say that the problem is classism and poverty, I tell you that a lot of disparities in health exist even after researchers adjust for income and whether or not someone has health insurance.

As an illustration, recall that some were surprised to hear that Serena Williams had to fight to get life-saving care after she gave birth to her healthy daughter. Serena is an internationally known professional tennis phenom. While you might assume that she would consistently receive world-class health care, you would be wrong. Following the birth of her daughter, she diagnosed herself with life-threatening blood clots and had to convince the medical staff (while out of breath) that they needed to conduct specific tests and intervene. She knew her body and her medical history, and she likely saved her *own* life.

This should not have happened. So many Black women have died in the fight, unsure if they were being too sensitive or misinterpreting their health concerns. Unfortunately, we fail to understand how much race and racism impact our well-being. It frustrates me when people argue that class supersedes racism. Poor Black folks have a hard time. Middle-class Black folks have more "means" but are still subjected to racial discrimination. If a Black Harvard professor can be detained while entering his own home because his neighbors believe that he does not belong, income and status help but do not protect Black people from racism.

Fight On with Knowledge

I would love to exist in a society where I do not have to explain to my seven-year-old son why a president hates him or anticipate years ahead when we have to teach him how to "survive the encounter" with police. I would rather not have to think about speaking standard English for fear of how I will be perceived if I used my more comfortable African American vernacular. I would love to imagine that you did not have to think about whether you can grow out your natural hair or how you can wear your hair if it is already natural. Imagine that you did not have to act like you were not shoplifting in a department store when you know that you are not.

But the reality is that every time I am in Waller County, where Sandra Bland was first pulled over, I have to pace my breathing to counteract my body's natural response to threatening circumstances. Our bodies do not know if the threat is real. It only matters if some situation is *perceived* as threatening. Racism and threats of racism keep us feeling unsafe and in danger. Our bodies are not designed to remain in fight-or-flight mode. This chronic state leads to physical and mental health problems for Black people. You may not have to drive down

Sandra Bland Parkway, but there are other threats that you encounter. Over time, the effects are detrimental.

I hope that sharing knowledge with you and others will lead to a movement of Black men and women who successfully operate in a less-than-affirming society, armed with knowledge rather than waiting for things to change. Conscious African Americans survive while having the ingenuity to maintain a dual mind—as Black and as African in America. This is nothing new. It is a survival strategy that I subscribe to because of my reality as a Black woman who professionally navigates primarily white spaces. These spaces presume to be "color-blind," but the drive to be color-blind seems to be the excuse that those in power use to deny racism. In doing so, racism is allowed to persist.

What this looks like is this: Racist thing happens; white person says, "I'm not racist," and asserts that they do not see color so they cannot possibly be racist; Black person is left questioning if the racist thing happened. White person goes on about their racist ways. If you have ever spent time in a color-blind workplace, it feels inauthentic. There is some mental disorder activated as well because if I am Black, but someone says, "I don't see you as Black," there is a problem. I feel confident that when Rev. Dr. Martin Luther King Jr. indicated that he did not want for his children to be judged by the color of their skin, he was not requesting that people not actually see the skin color that is staring them in the face.

I recognize that I may have unearthed some realities that you would rather forget. You may have been benefiting from your own defense mechanisms that have permitted you to function in your daily life without the burden of racism. All is not lost. My goal is to bring some things to light so you can understand that the problem is not you.

You and maybe your loved ones are up against someone else's insanity. However, that insanity has persisted for so long because so many have denied that it existed. Now that you are more aware about the validity of your daily experience of racism, you can be more intentional about the decisions you make and your efforts to strengthen your PF.

Fortunately, there is research suggesting that when you have a positive sense of who you are, the threats matter less. Self-affirming messages about your ability to withstand threats to who you are can be very effective. Another important detail to consider is that you are not in this alone. An African proverb says, "When spiderwebs unite, they can tie up a lion."

CHAPTER 6

Assimilating and Internalizing Racism

Middle-class and affluent Black families navigate considerable obstacles on the road to the "American Dream." Perhaps with the exception of church, extended family get-togethers, and Jack and Jill events, these families spend most of their time in primarily white environments—work, school, and after-school activities—where they are expected to fit in. Assimilation means taking on a culture that is not your own to avoid seeming threatening. Doing so requires accepting that your ideas, culture, preferences, and concerns fall to the wayside. You must learn to carry yourself in a way that is acceptable to white society rather than inherent to your culture. This poses an ongoing psychological conundrum about who you are that challenges your PF. The promise of assimilation is that we can have it all, but we lose our mind.

Fitting In, Unnaturally So

You already know what it looks like to be "acceptable." You are curious about the natural hair movement, but you can't wear your hair to work like that. You have gotten so comfortable with being *un*natural that you cannot fathom leaving your house without your wig. Maybe you ventured to wear your hair curly one day, followed by a flat iron a few days later, only to have several coworkers comment, "Oh, I like your hair better like that." They won't let you be natural! Really, they won't. The workplace is one of the biggest challenges overall. Recognizing that you might bring "attention" to yourself, you avoid being seen too often with the only other Black person whose office is on your floor. You are also sure to code-switch, speaking your best Standard American English rather than the African American Vernacular English that you speak at home and likely spoke growing up.

Crossing Barriers Can Be Disruptive

We're usually pretty good at separating our comfortable vernacular from our mainstream vernacular, but I witnessed a hilarious incident when I was a high schooler working at a very popular local, family-owned restaurant in Savannah, Georgia. The family owners were white, but all of the kitchen staff were Black women. You know the scene. I would estimate that the "baby" of the cooks was about fifty years old. I enjoyed those ladies. Their joking and teasing with one another while handling business in the kitchen reminded me of time spent with my aunts and uncles and cousins out in the "country." Important work in the kitchen mixed with laughter and easiness.

It is this easiness that Black people get to enjoy when there are no white folks around. It was fascinating that the ladies in the kitchen pulled off the easiness so frequently because there was a revealing window opening that separated them from the takeout counter. The takeout window was where they passed food to one of the owner's two sons, who were always present, overseeing things.

Well one day, the younger, more lighthearted son somewhat chastised the senior cook about how she put something on a plate. Without missing a step, she said, "I ain't studdin' you!" Everything was fine until he tried to repeat what she said, but with confusion: "What'd you say? You ain't...what?" In that moment, she realized that she'd brought her kitchen easiness to someone who wasn't supposed to understand. He was amused and confused all at the same time.

I was fascinated by the short standoff. She didn't translate, and he didn't understand. You either don't use your vernacular with white people or you use it with white people that understand so you don't have to stop the usual rhythm and flow to explain. Even if you're the family member who doesn't get all of the inside jokes, you know the language. You've known it your entire life. It is one thing that separates you from white folks, but it's so second nature that you don't think anything of it. You only know that you don't have the same "ease" in white spaces as you do when you get to just show up as you.

We Navigate Horrifying Racial Realities

Did you see the movie *Get Out?* The movie is a cultural phenomenon. I mention it here because Chris, the main character, is well aware of his Blackness and how he has to navigate the world as a Black man. In a nutshell, it's a horror film about white racism.

Chris visits his white girlfriend's family for the first time during a weekend getaway. Prior to visiting his girlfriend's parents, he asks if her parents even know that he is Black. He was acutely aware of what it meant that she was taking him home to her white family. When they were stopped by a police officer along the way, he complied with the officer who unjustly asked for his identification. He knows how to survive encounters, but he was willing to participate in the look-who's-coming-to-dinner occasion as part of the next stage of a relationship with his white girlfriend. Throughout the movie, we see his good sense telling him to pay attention, ask questions, and not accept things as they are.

Chris was obviously a Black man with awareness of the world around him. I wonder what the decisions were that he made and what he convinced himself of in his mind to end up in such circumstances. Don't get me wrong. Love has no boundaries. However, he was clearly very apprehensive about the family visit and chose to press on in the interest of his relationship. He bought in to her reassurance that everything would be fine. Yet, how often do situations like this turn out to be "all good" to you?

Going into the situation, Chris could not have conceived of a scenario whereby wypipo literally steal his talents and body for their own purposes and amusement. Could you imagine a scenario where this has happened for countless Black men and women? Who would think up such a thing—and under the guise of innocence? It's a good thing he shut that whole scene down, using his own brilliance to fight the sunken place, to fight for his life, and to get out. I share this to say that, while assimilation smooths out our differences for white people, it is closer to a horror show that we live daily. This twisting who we are undermines our PF. Even knowing that our Blackness is falling under a white gaze or worse, being used as that gaze chooses, hurts our mental health.

Assimilation Is Not an Answer to the Fortitude Problem

Some Black people can thrive in predominantly white school and work environments that do not affirm them. I say "some" because if you were one of them, you would not be so far through this book. You are either not in a predominantly white work setting, you recognize that you are not thriving, or you are realizing at this very moment that you must not be thriving. In any case, valuing assimilation over Black identity works out just fine for some. Some degree of assimilation (i.e., participation) in this current society is necessary, but we have to be very intentional.

When my husband and I moved to Georgia for new faculty appointments, we had not been married for very long but hoped to start our family soon. The realtor asked what was important to us, and we mentioned close proximity to the university and good schools. You can likely relate to wanting that balance between not having a long commute and making sure that the schools are "good." Part of the natural order for Black parents is to have to negotiate "good" versus "diverse and relatable" when deciding what is most important for our children.

Since my husband and I mentioned that schools were important, the realtor took us to a coveted neighborhood that had a high-performing school district. That neighborhood might have been just fine. Those white neighbors who stared at us uncomfortably were very likely good people. We, however, were not willing to invest our hard-earned money into finding out if they would be "tolerant." For us, the gamble on whether the neighbors and their children would be accepting was not worth the risk. It is a sad reality.

You may have faced the city-to-suburb dilemma. You and your spouse moved to a suburb so your son and daughter could have the best possible education in a "safe" environment. Perhaps your family is the only Black family on your street, and there are maybe two other Black families altogether in the surrounding neighborhood. You liked your old neighborhood that was mostly Black families, but the schools were "average performing," with too many behavior and discipline problems. To provide the best for your children, you and your husband agreed to move. You could not take the chance that your future college-bound children would be bullied or subjected to teachers who would not help them reach their full potential. The best answer, you believed, was to find a neighborhood in a competitive school district or enroll your child in an expensive 90 percent white Christian academy. Your decision may have put your daughter in the best school, but she has to deal with being "the only one." You tell yourself that others have done it; she will be fine. But I would like to suggest a different, psychological fortitude-driven approach.

Weighing the Realities with Your Options

One thing that my husband and I will always agree on is the value of neighborhoods where the schools are perceived by some to be "not-so-good." These schools tend to have more Black students enrolled. Our child is also less likely, in these schools, to fall into the margins of identity—ambivalent or not knowing who he is as a Black person. We do not expect that Black people are all the same, but we do know that being "the only one" can wreak havoc on how our son sees himself, how much self-hate he internalizes, and whether or not he has opportunities to connect with others who value being Black.

Let's say your son has a psychological fortitude rating of 99. Nothing, and certainly not racism or systemic oppression, can rattle him. Maybe he fits in well and isn't perceived as threatening. This could all be true, but it is rare that children in these predominantly white settings do not suffer the isolation and hits to self-esteem that result. I do not believe it to be worth the risk to find out later in life that he was holding on by a thread because he knew that he was expected to do well at that high-performing school where his humanity was questioned or he was constantly treated as the "other."

Do you know the analogy of the frog in the pot? It acclimates to an increasingly hotter temperature of water until it is cooked. Your daughter does her best to manage subtle slights about her hair, complexion, and acting "uppity" until one day it's just too much.

If your daughter ends up in a difficult situation whereby she doesn't fit in as the only Black girl, but is fortified with the knowledge that she comes from people who have tremendous achievements, she can better withstand the assaults to her psychological fortitude. On the other hand, if she identifies with a less spiritual culture, one in which the individual and not God is responsible for life, suicide may be a viable solution for unending pain. A popular African proverb says that "I am because we are." In an Africentric worldview, God is responsible for life and the individual exists most importantly as part of a larger *community*.

Culture Is Important When Assimilation Comes with Side Effects

There is no way to conduct the type of research that would allow me to say definitively that Black culture prevents suicide in Black people. I do think, however, that the research (and you would say your common sense) shows us enough to make certain predictions. Imagine that two unrelated, same-age, heterosexual Black men (we'll call them JT and Bret) endure several years of tragedy: their fiancées die in a tragic accident in 2012, they lose everything in the stock market the next year, they are denied promotion while a white colleague's promotion goes through with flying colors. JT has a strong sense of African or Black identity (even if he doesn't know to call it that). Bret "is his own man."

You hear a news report that one of them died by suicide. Suicide is very complex, so either one of them could have elevated risk. Based on my research, however, I would predict that JT would not have taken his own life. We do not know why, but we do know that something about cultural connection builds endurance in the face of tragedy.

It is okay to move to the suburbs or enroll your child in a high-performing school if, and only if, you are prepared to empower children with all of the Wakandan energy that you can muster.

The Effects of Isolation on Mental Health

Assimilation may seem like an easy trade-off in the context of school and work because when you are immersed in the majority culture, it feels like you are just going with the flow. But we sometimes discover over time that the sacrifice of self and culture required to fit in and be included has a high cost. It feels like mere inconveniences that Black people encounter—at least it's not slavery. But the weight of these inconveniences accumulates over time. Before you know it, you break down under the pressure. Moving with the flow but away from family to pursue a "better life" means that your children lose access to the family stories of unconditional love, determination, and family pride. While assimilation can make life easier, it can also lead to serious emotional health problems, such as the constant fear of rejection, subtle and overt exclusion, and microaggressions that are all part of a racist world. The families, adults and children alike, in these settings experience real assaults on their psychological fortitude.

You have separated yourself from the cultural comforts that help combat these assaults: time with extended family, culture-based traditions, and activities that are sown into Black music and art (all resources for PF that we'll soon dive into). As a result of your separation, you can become increasingly vulnerable to anxiety, depression, and a slew of psychological problems and conditions. To add, you may even begin to view Black people through the racist lens that surrounds you.

Dr. Na'im Akbar, a preeminent scholar in African psychology, would say that the inclination to value what white folks value to the exclusion of Black/African culture is a sign of an "alien-self disorder." When we as Black people work collectively toward the survival of Black people, those values and beliefs reflect psychological strength and well-being—order and not *disorder*. If you insist that "time is money" rather than "I am because we are," you may have adopted a way of seeing the world that is more consistent with a European perspective. If you know a Black person who subscribes to a mentality that Black people are subhuman (in the way that some white people insist), that individual is afflicted by what Akbar would say is "anti-self disorder." These afflictions are a consequence of living in a society that teaches us (and everyone else) that Black people have no value.

Your Risk for Internalizing Racism Increases

Before we dive into ways to immerse yourself in cultural traditions that affirm who you are, I want to address how much you are immersed in a reality that does the opposite and sets your psychological fortitude back. If your mind "does not see color," I am surprised that you have read this far. The hard reality I want to reinforce is that you cannot reclaim your mind and be "culture-neutral" at the same time.

I know that mainstream society has tried to convince you that we are all the same and that Black people who "make everything about race" are the real problem. This is an opinion. I know that it can be intimidating to examine and rethink your current reality. You probably had some clues that you were operating in an alternate reality, perhaps even a fake reality, but could not quite put your finger on the "it" that drove this underlying suspicion. The "it" is that your ancestors had to hide who they were in order to survive. By hiding the true African self over generations, you inherited the story that you are just American or that being African American is just about your skin color. I stumbled across a profound meme online that said, "To be African American is to be African with no memory and to be American with no privilege."

Many of us are aware that we lack white privileges relative to others, but very few of us are aware of our absent memory.

Take a moment to get real. Only you need to know this, so be honest with yourself. Then, answer these questions.

On a scale from 0 to 100, with 100 meaning that you absolutely believe this statement, rate how much you believe the following statements:

- Black people are inherently not as smart as white people.

- Black people who have light skin and eyes are more attractive than Black people who have darker skin and eyes.

- Black people are inherently more criminal than white people.

This is a crude approach, but if your rating falls in the range of 50 to 100 on any one of these statements, you will benefit from reeducating yourself. You have internalized some notion that white people are superior to Black people, so you have made—and will continue to make—decisions based on this belief. The truth you need to discover for yourself is that Black people may do things differently, but this is a difference and not a deficiency. The characteristics that make us different are rooted in something deeply creative and unique, so we do not have to be limited by others' imaginations.

If you add your three scores and divide by three to achieve a crude racism self-assessment score that is 15 to 49, you will still benefit from some reorientation. Mainstream society is constantly reinforcing that racial differences are due to the inferiority of Black people. It is almost everywhere we look, from the challenges that have arisen in the Black community due in large part to attempts to overcome systemic racism, to the health care system that creates severe mistrust in us, to the injustice system with its many layers that cause problems for Black people just going about daily life. These challenges will take time to overcome, even within yourself. So I strongly encourage you to recognize your internalized racism and how it impacts your thinking and behavior on an ongoing basis. And always seek new ways to bolster who you are as an African-descended person.

Why We Proclaim "Wakanda Forever!"

When was the last time that you saw yourself and people who looked like you tapping into their brilliance without having to bend to what was acceptable and less Black? The manner in which we see ourselves directly impacts our mood, thinking, self-esteem, aspirational goals, and vision. The people perish without a vision. You may have to intentionally seek more opportunities to see Black people engaged in inspiring art and innovation beyond sports and music. Doing so can indirectly improve your overall confidence and well-being as you see people who look like you creating new avenues for success.

Whether or not you saw the groundbreaking movie *Black Panther*, you witnessed the excitement that African Americans experienced. The movie was directed by Ryan Coogler, an accomplished African American director, producer, and screenwriter who also cowrote the film's screenplay. The film told the comic-inspired story of the Black Panther superhero of Wakanda, a technologically advanced African kingdom.

Almost all of the main cast were Black. It was awe-inspiring. I never imagined that a movie could have such a deep impact on Black people. We were coordinating African attire and putting on our own social media productions. I, too, went out and got a new outfit for the occasion. But our clothing wasn't the whole story. "Wakanda forever" became a unifying new mantra for African people, including African Americans, around the world. We know what it means when we say "Wakanda forever!" with pride and enthusiasm. *Black Panther* was everything, and there is a reason why.

If you saw the film, it may have transported you to a place that spoke to your soul. Beautiful, heroic, creative, loyal people were on full display. We saw ourselves in the most positive and perhaps even unimaginable (for some) light. In the movie, women were not subordinate. They were brilliant. They were in charge. It was an amusing highlight of the movie when the young sister so naturally referred to "the colonizer." In Wakanda, Black people were in charge of everything, including what the world knew about them. They knew who they were.

At times, they were uncompromising so they could ensure their survival.

It is notable that, in *Black Panther*, the main antagonist was complicated—he had good intentions to free his Black people, but he was misguided. Remember, "all your skinfolk ain't your kinfolk." Having the family "key" made him "look" like family, but his method was mired in a Eurocentric, survival-of-the-fittest way of seeing the world. This is true for some who look African but are misguided and have adopted mainstream ways that are destructive to Africans. In the end, we saw his wisdom. When he asked Black Panther to "just bury me in the ocean with my ancestors who jumped from ships, 'cause they knew death was better than bondage," it was a declaration that hit home in our current land of bondage. You may have heard some of the real stories of Africans who jumped overboard to their deaths rather than be subjected to inhumane treatment. This was more than a line from a superhero movie. It connected fiction to the history and reality of African people all over the world.

If you feel you are drowning in any of the psychological problems I have described in these past chapters, it is high time you connect to the source of the psychological fortitude that can get you through. Connecting with who you are, genuinely (not limited by myths of the "dark continent"), can help you recover the resourcefulness you need to build a life worth living and passing on to future generations.

Envision your community as one where children are nurtured by their teachers; where little Black girls are inspired to explore science with their boldest imaginations; where your young adult brother doesn't give a second thought to the police lights behind in his rearview mirror; where Grandma can get checked into the hospital and get the same smile, care, and concern as the white woman patient in the room next door; where your cousin runs for office where voting isn't impacted by suspicious identification laws or voting machines; and where you have the psychological fortitude to develop and patent your best idea yet. Imagine a day in the life of such a community. If such a vision seems far-fetched, imagine it for your son's generation.

For your lifetime, you can imagine a workplace where you unapologetically celebrate your coworker-sista's success the way Taraji Henson so enthusiastically cheered for Viola Davis when Ms. Davis became the first Black woman to get the Emmy for her lead role in a drama. Taraji was nominated in the same category, but her excitement for Viola's win was beautiful to witness. We will have competition and occasional conflicts, but neither has to rival our sisterhoods or our vision for our communities.

PART II RECLAIM YOUR MIND TO RECLAIM A LIFE WORTH LIVING

CHAPTER 7

Exploring and Expanding
Meaningful Blackness

Many of us have joined the trend of getting genetics testing. My analysis did not reveal more about my ancestry than I assumed before the results arrived. I had some inkling that my roots were primarily in West Africa. Most enslaved people in the colonies came from West African countries, including present-day Senegal, Gambia, Mali, Angola, Congo, the Democratic Republic of Congo, Gabon, Ghana, and Cameroon. When I traveled to Ghana as a graduate student, I was assumed to be Ghanaian as long as I kept my mouth shut.

While I don't have a well-formed theory on our genetic fascination, I do believe that by knowing our ancestry, we gain feelings of connection and a sense of place in the world—a place that goes beyond chattel slavery. At the same time, I want to point out what you may not realize: you already have that connection within your very being. And your identity as a person of African descent can unlock your psychological fortitude. "Africanisms" are those cultural words, actions, spirituality, and ways of seeing the world that are unique to us as African-descended people. They have been passed down to each of us, from generation to generation and family to family, and they have now reached you.

There is an African proverb that says, "No matter how long a log stays in the water, it doesn't become a crocodile." To me, it means that no matter how much of your identity has been robbed or your family's generations of captivity, you will always be African.

My research shows that African Americans who do not see their Black selves in a positive way are at an increased risk for suicide. On the other hand, a positive connection to Black identity protects us to some degree through psychological "buffers." When you have a buffer, bad things can happen, but they do not have as much of a negative effect on you compared to someone who does not have a buffer.

This is part of the many reasons that I urge you to prioritize your psychological fortitude by intentionally connecting with your authentic identity. This connection can reinforce your own well-being in addition to passing on strategies for resilience for the next generation. This chapter is filled with ideas for how you can connect with the cultural enrichment that, when made a part of daily life now, can cascade far into your family's future and for generations to come.

You Can Access Wakandan Energy by Being Who You Are

My research is part of a consistent body of work that insists Black people generally do better when connected to their own culture. Being connected to your Africanness is good for your well-being and also good for children's self-esteem and success in school. It is not a direct cause-and-effect, but a good sense of self seems to be correlated with success in life—they go together. Conversely, if you do not have a positive impression of Black people, when ignorant messages show up, you are at risk for believing them.

Here's how this works. Say you are really good at baking cakes. You know beyond a shadow of a doubt that you are good. Someone comes along and says, "Your cakes aren't that good." You might think, *Maybe this cake didn't come out the best, but I know I can show out in the kitchen.* Now, imagine that you're a so-so kind of cook, but you were asked to bake for the church anniversary. You overhear someone saying your cake was dry. It bothers you because you didn't believe that you were a good cook anyway, but you agreed to provide a dessert to help the event. If your psychological fortitude is already hovering around a 40, you are even more susceptible to what you overhear. If your level is high, then you will think about the criticism briefly, but not for long. This scenario is just about cooking—what happens when the issue is a deeper one that really hits home?

Now, let's imagine that you secretly believe that you are not "as Black" as your darker-skinned siblings because of your complexion. Because they teased you relentlessly as a child, you have always struggled with your identity. Though your mother chastised them for teasing you, she never talked to you (or your siblings) about the many beautiful complexions of African people. When the guy at the bar makes an unexpected comment about how he usually likes women with a darker complexion, you bristle for reasons you cannot explain. On the other hand, if you know that your lighter complexion says nothing about who you are, his ignorance is meaningless.

You might be tempted to raise your children to be "color-blind" or "race-neutral" in an attempt to save them from developing self-limiting ideas and behavior. If your child is biracial, it is unfair to raise them to "choose" one half of who they are. However, telling your child that "race does not matter as long as they work hard" is only true until it matters. If your child looks like a person of color, they are likely to experience racial bias in the United States. Such bias and potential mistreatment can be very disturbing for a child or young adult who has no perspective from which to understand this biased reality. It might be nice to not have "labels." When the time comes that Black women are no longer fighting to survive childbirth and Black men are no longer gunned down in the streets by police or any self-deputized overseers, I will be the first to sign up to be label-free.

Racial socialization is an important part of what it means to be Black. If a Black child does not have a positive Black identity to navigate his world, he may encounter considerable emotional turmoil. Where does he fit in? The identity struggle can be difficult to navigate. Be strategic and intentional as you help your child navigate the strange world. Race relations are complex, so internalizing beliefs that white people are all bad or that Black people are lazy will not be helpful.

Your Black ancestors surrendered their cultural identity long ago to survive. They would have *gladly* maintained their uncolonized heritage. You have been willingly struggling to get your son to "fit in" to the colonizer's system. Meanwhile, he is marginalized, feels justifiably unsafe, and never believes he quite belongs. This lack of belonging can have emotional consequences.

Why Reclaim? Because Your Identity Was Stolen and It's Time to Get You Back

I choose the word "reclaim" to suggest that we must retrieve or recover something from someone. Congresswoman Maxine Waters, aka Auntie Maxine, famously used the word "reclaiming" during a congressional hearing in 2017. Each congressperson has limited time to address important issues during a congressional hearing. Congresswoman Waters asked Treasury Secretary Steven Mnuchin a direct question, which he attempted to avoid by answering with long-winded, superficial compliments to the Congresswoman. Auntie could have said, "Please don't waste my time." Instead, she went further, she wanted to go on record, so she repeated the phrase, "Reclaiming my time," over and over again until she was given the floor back. The Congresswoman never willingly gave up her time. There was, however, an attempt to take it from her.

Just as Auntie Maxine reclaimed each minute that belonged to her before someone else could take it over with his agenda, we must each reclaim our mind after it was stolen when our culture was stolen. But reclaiming a cultural identity is just the first step: we also need to look at what Black people have been through in the United States (and beyond) and the ways we have survived—both for the better and for the worse. We need to do this for ourselves and on behalf of our families.

Our battles with racism are centuries old and have taken multitudes of forms in history, headlines, and daily life. The core reason why racism has been so destructive is that it denies who we are. As a result, we label individual acts of brilliance and success as Black girl magic or Black boy joy rather than embracing that this is who we are when not relegated to the boot of oppression.

Dr. Asa Hilliard was a professor of educational psychology who studied and taught indigenous ancient African history, culture, education, and society. His "Free Your Mind" lectures made this point so eloquently.[30] He described how, for African people to be controlled, our memory had to be erased and our culture suppressed. Then we were relentlessly socialized to believe that white people are superior. This notion of the absolute superiority of white over Black was legally sanctioned as Black people were excluded from the population and not guaranteed access to basic human rights, such as education, economic independence, and protection by laws. The laws have changed, but the exclusions still exist.

Professional football in the United States seems to offer the clearest example of how Black people are undervalued and have embraced this status. For years, football leagues prevented Black men from playing the game professionally. Even today, the quarterback position is believed to be suited for white men only. With today's record number of Black men at the quarterback position, the historical lag time and the elevated scrutiny of Black quarterbacks in college football and in the NFL has been, and is, by racist design.

In pro football, Black men easily outnumber white male players, coaches, and "owners" in the same way that enslaved Africans outnumbered white people in South Carolina in the 1700s. Because "players" do not individually embrace their collective power, they remain players rather than decision makers. It is historically true that once we get our hands on something, things change. I encourage you to research the many examples of this, but for now I'll say that if your five-star son and all his friends and their friends played football at historically Black universities like Prairie View rather than Texas A&M, we would begin to see a shift. If we decide to take back some of our power, we would realize our own lucrative football league.

Of course, this is easier said than done. Making sacrifices to overcome many generations of psychological enslavement is not easy given the predicament we are in. How can the psychologically enslaved dig ourselves out from the generations of dysfunction that we have had to endure? As W. E. B. Du Bois said in 1909, "The cost of liberty is less than the price of repression," and this applies today.[31] In order for your family to be controlled, on a daily basis, you must stay ignorant of who you truly are, relegate African culture to food and music, never identify with or band together in community, and don't buy ice from Black people because you've bought into the notion that white people's ice is colder. Just as your football-playing son will have to recognize his own repression in the game, you, yourself, cannot expect real change while accepting an inferior place in life.

Over time, you gave up your own mind by assuming that if you could fit into white people's world, you would be a better person. You passed this on to your children. You didn't intentionally communicate that *white is right*, but you kind of did. As a result, your children show up in places, like my classroom, suggesting that they're just American, believing that there is limited value in being seen as Black and that Blackness is a liability.

Reclaim Your Right to See Yourself as African

Black psychologists have conducted numerous studies that show that when Black men, women, and children have a positive sense of who we are as Black people, we thrive in quality of life and overall well-being. There seems to be an undeniable connection between being in touch with your Blackness, and specifically your Africanness, and your psychological fortitude. The tragedy of this is that, if you have tried to move your family away from the "poorer" environment where you grew up toward the mainstream, upper middle-income society that you have earned, you may have inadvertently created new problems.

Asa Hilliard famously posed the query, "to be African or not to be," which speaks to the dire need for your authenticity as a person of African ancestry.[32] Your only choice for living a full life is to live as a person of African descent, connecting to an African culture and sense of community. Hilliard's assertion invokes one of Shakespeare's tragedies for our purposes—one in which the main character, Hamlet, wrestles with the idea of suicide. For Hamlet, suicide would not be so bad if it rids him of his suffering. The "To be?" question points to the urgency of survival.

If being African seems radical to you, I submit that only a radical disposition will move you forward. When people say that they "don't see you as Black," how does that make you feel? It is usually meant as a compliment. Do you see it that way? I can see how you might. The person is usually trying to say that they are not prejudiced or racist. They may be trying to say that you don't carry yourself with any of the stereotypical Black behavior. But if your psychological fortitude were solid, you would be offended that the individual takes issue with Black people. This same strong psychological fortitude would also allow you to move past their comment with the knowledge that this is the individual's problem and not yours.

Watch the movie *Sankofa*, a fictional account of a Black model who unexpectedly finds herself back in time and enslaved. Watch it with your parents and grandparents or anyone from a generation older than yours, if you can. See the horrors of captivity (though I caution that the horror includes violence against the main character). See also the sense of community reflected in what you see in your family and families that you grew up with. These stories are rarely visited so we can "move on," but we cannot move on from our very culture and our understanding of how it came to be. The word "Sankofa" comes from a Ghanaian language that means "to go back and get it." It is represented by the symbol of a mythical bird with its head turned backward. The idea of Sankofa is that you must reclaim and preserve your past in order to have a productive future.

Reclaim Our History

Dr. Asa Hilliard hit the mark when he pointed out that our lack of historical knowledge disables us. We must begin to challenge what we think we know about ourselves. This is why an important step in your rehabilitation is to read the truth about yourself in texts that expose you to both ancient and contemporary history. Here are some places to start:

- Read about what the (Black) Moors contributed to European civilization.

- We are not taught in most schools that all of humanity descended from an African woman. Can you imagine what that would do for your daughter's self-esteem to know this? Read Cheikh Anta Diop's *The African Origin of Civilization: Myth or Reality*.

- Read Carter G. Woodson's *Miseducation of the Negro* to begin to understand how Black people came to be so systematically lost, cooked like frogs in indoctrinating schools.

- Read Dr. Na'im Akbar's *Breaking the Chains of Psychological Slavery* to understand how oppression has infiltrated our minds.

Reclaim Our Hair and Our Language

While you're out claiming things, you might as well reclaim your hair and your language. Two things that we find ourselves referring to as "bad" are "bad hair" and "bad English." In recent years, tremendous positive energy has shifted toward valuing our natural hair. One of my favorite moments in the *Black Panther* movie was when Okoye, the general of the Wakanda armed forces, complained about the wig that she wore as a disguise. She said it was a disgrace. Frankly, some of the feats that Black women go through to look less African and more European are a disgrace.

You might argue that blond hair and colored contacts are not about any kind of self-hate. Instead, you thought the lighter eyes were pretty. You may even describe naturally kinky hair as "bad" hair. This is one of those things that you will have to give up. Go cold turkey. The only good hair is the hair that is growing healthily out of your head. Now, you might work in a corporate setting where you would be frowned upon if you wear your natural hair. This is what you have told yourself.

The truth is that until you step out in your natural hair, you do not know what the response will be. If straight hair is not part of the dress code, your own natural hair is fair game. It is all part of embracing a new mind-set so you can elevate your psychological fortitude. You cannot do so by putting harsh chemicals on your head. Also, you cannot show your daughter how she can love her hair when you refuse to leave the house without one of your wigs. Part of the reason that the *Black Panther* movie resonated was the unapologetically African imagery. There was no straight hair. There was only natural beauty. If you are not comfortable with your hair, that is completely understandable. You can begin by asking yourself what you are telling yourself about your hair.

Our natural hair is not the only way that we malign our natural way of being. Part of Black culture is how we talk. Unfortunately, we have labeled much of our speech as "bad English." I remember my mother breaking me out of the habit of saying "my sister, she..." It seemed natural to me, but not to my mom, who believed that the insertion of that extra "she" was "bad English." But how we talk is part of who we are! 50 Cent with no *s*. That's African. Read Geneva Smitherman's *Talkin' and Testifyin'*. The missing *g*'s—that's African. It is not lazy-talk. But like you, I was conditioned to how we are "supposed" to talk to keep from "sounding ignorant."

This point about language is an example that illustrates how you have been brainwashed to buy into African inferiority. Meanwhile, Black people are out here surviving brilliantly. Most of us use African American Vernacular English (AAVE). Of course we use slang, but AAVE is not slang or lazy. Even if she "ain't never" on time, it's not bad English. It is governed by a West African grammar structure and English words for a people who were self-taught in horrid conditions and were segregated far longer than integrated. Putting our culture down for surviving will compromise your authenticity and your well-being. Code-switching, when you shift from your more comfortable African American vernacular to Standard American English, is understandable. However, rejecting Black English as ghetto or slang is problematic. You have to shift how you think about the legitimacy of Black people beyond sports and other forms of entertainment.

Reclaim Black Culture Beyond "American"

You already know that your spirituality is a huge part of your culture. Lord knows that you would not have survived this long with your mind partly intact if you did not have a strong sense of faith in God, passed down to you from generation to generation. This is the thing about culture—we learn who we are from the previous generation. In the same way, if you pass on to your children that they are "just American," they lose their true identity. You must intentionally label that which is "African" so your son does not have to rely on others to give him positive messages about who he is.

Black culture is African in origin. If you recoil from this truth, if you are uncomfortable with your connection to Africa, you would greatly benefit from a reintroduction to your Motherland. Do not filter it through the racist American lens that would have us willingly separate ourselves from the richness, and depth of beauty and excellence, that being African holds for us. So I will say again, Black culture is African because your ancestors brought their culture from various places mostly in West Africa. They did not bring their culture from Europe. African culture is distinct and it is brilliant and it was preserved in ways you do not know because our habits were not attributed to Africa. We adapted to our circumstances, but the foundation is African.

Just because the only thing that you learned about Black culture in history class was slavery does not mean that there isn't so much more to who Black people are. The stories of what we have achieved are limitless! Even during slavery, Black culture was preserved because we were isolated. We act as if Black folks arrived in the United States on the *Niña*, *Pinta*, and *Santa Maria* and immediately became "Americanized." Think about this: Even though there were some "house Negroes," your ancestors were almost completely isolated from the mainstream colonizers. They therefore maintained what they could of their culture. This isolation was pretty much intact through 1965 due to Jim Crow Laws and legal separation.

Yes, your ancestors were kidnapped, exploited, and convinced that they were not human. Successful Black communities were tormented and burned to the ground. This is the legacy that endures to this day. It did not end with our kidnapping or burn with Black Wall Street in 1921. Fortunately, you are looking for answers—deeper answers that have meaning for your life, for those who you care about, and for those who are tired of being on the wrong side of justice. I'm sorry the answer is not easy. If you need a deeper answer, you will have to find it in recognizing your strengths as a person of African descent.

Reclaim by Imagining Your Ancestors' True Stories

If your family participates in family reunions, use those occasions to talk to older family members about what your family was like before you were born. Older family members are living history. What was life like for them growing up? What kinds of things did people do for one another that they miss in their neighborhood now? Are there any family stories that they hold?

Imagine you have an ancestor who lived so long ago that no one alive in your family can trace your roots to her. In Ghana, she was Ada, which means "first daughter." Your ancestors were very intentional about naming traditions. Names had meaning often linked to the infant's spirit, the situation surrounding the infant's birth, or perhaps the day of the week. In West Africa, we had names that had meaning. Perhaps your parents gave you a name that would allow you to fit in, but you gave your daughter an African name that has meaning, like Nia or Asha.

In Ghana, your ancestral grandmother Ada lived in a community with her sisters and their children and families. Some of her sisters were actually cousins, but there was no language or distinction for "cousins." They were sisters and brothers. Everyone looked out for one another.

Individuals survived because they were part of a community that worked together. They got what was needed from the nearby land. They had chores and responsibilities, but no one was in a hurry when they spent time talking about the day or a struggle. Time wasn't about the clock, but it was about being present for a neighbor and honoring and learning from the past. The distant future did not matter as much as the present. No place was more important than where they were. The importance of family, Ada's protectiveness of her play-cousins who weren't even blood relatives, and her strong connection to a Higher Power—these are part of your cultural heritage that was passed on.

Twenty-three-year-old Ada did not need to "escape" her home outside of Kumasi, Ghana. She was very happy and had everything that she needed. If you have ever visited the continent, you may have been surprised to see that people who have a fraction of the means that you have are very content. The children are happy and smiling. They know who they are, and they have what they need. They are anxious for nothing and have every confidence that God will provide. Those who would say that Ada was better off in the United States have fed you a lie: contemporary research shows that spending time in the United States, even now, is psychologically toxic for people of color.[33]

Ada managed to survive ten weeks in the bottom of a ship. Her two youngest children did not. Once she arrived in Charleston, she did her best to survive. She learned to communicate with other kidnapped Africans. Both her husband and her two older children were separated from her. She did not know where she was or what to do, but she knew that she had to survive to see her husband and children again. When she was taken to a large plantation in Georgia, older Black women did their best to communicate with her. She learned nouns and verbs and could eventually speak and understand well enough. Life was hard, but her belief in the Divine was the one thing that remained with her. The circumstances were dire, but her beliefs gave her the will to fight another day.

Your great-great-grandmother, Elizabeth, was a descendent of Ada's. Ms. Elizabeth cleaned homes in Atlanta. She went to church regularly and prayed to God to keep her children safe and a roof over their heads. She was everyone's auntie. Her children went to segregated schools, where they learned about the many accomplishments of Black scientists. The community was strong as long as they stood together. When her daughter participated in sit-ins at the local Woolworth, she prayed all night. Ms. Elizabeth never really believed that colored folks would be allowed to integrate lunch counters in Atlanta, but the boycotts had been successful in Alabama. She prayed for all of the protesters. But somehow, the civil rights movement ended without ever achieving equality. Your great-great-grandmother was so worn out that all she could do was to focus on getting her children an education.

Just a few generations from Ada, your intellectual and creative talents will advance your community and simultaneously increase your overall well-being. Storing up all your gifts for yourself is not why they were given to you. Living your purpose increases your psychological fortitude and contributes to the betterment of your community. Your objective for yourself is to redirect from "How can I make law partner?" to "How does making partner help my community?" Your objective is not to get as close to white people as possible, achieving individual wealth that in no way helps your community. Your objective is to walk your authentic life path. Remembering who Ada was and how she lived is a key to doing this.

Reclaim Our Stories

To be educated in a way that matters, you must accept that the way people talk in your community and their profound sense of creativity, style, and spirituality are no accident. Reclaiming your mind is planning potlucks with other families and also about forming book clubs to read books by Black authors that center on Black experiences. Here are three fictional options to put on your must-read list.

Chinua Achebe's *Things Fall Apart* is set in precolonial Nigeria and widely read throughout the world. It gives the reader an opportunity to see the imposition of the Western world through an African lens.

If you haven't read Toni Morrison's *Beloved*, or even if you have, you might consider it as a fictional account of slavery's impact on men, women, and families. Read it not for entertainment, but as an opportunity to revisit the atrocity of slavery.

Finally, Tomi Adeyemi's *Children of Blood and Bone* is a story that reflects beautiful imagery. The main character is an impressive Black girl. Story themes highlight Yoruba culture. If you did not look into Yoruba culture given the imagery in Beyonce's acclaimed *Lemonade* album, it is time to do some research. You are missing out on so much beauty and significance.

Consider each of these books not just as a fictional narrative but as representative of a culture to which you have been disconnected. You need to be very intentional about reclaiming your mind: it starts with self-educating and educating your children if they are not in an African-centered school. Reclaiming expands when you connect with like-minded Black people. Increasingly, you will have less tolerance for those who get together just to gossip. Some people gossip because it is the only way they know to manage their low PF. Leave them to it. If you already participate in monthly activities with book-club friends, neighbors, or church members, you might be able to do more even with this group— on a more meaningful level.

You Can Stand Firm on a Reclaimed Foundation

The racist system that we live in repeatedly and intentionally fails to affirm you. It has stolen your African identity so much so that you gladly relinquish it. Despite these realties, your creative style and capacity to improvise are part of what has allowed Black people to survive oppressive systems. Dr. James Jones, trustees' distinguished professor emeritus and director of the Center for the Study of Diversity at the University of Denver, explained our culture in part as a collective of spirituality, improvisation, and dedication to oral, in-person communication. If you pay attention, you can identify your own examples of

African American improvisation and creativity in response to the problem of everyday discrimination.

An example that comes to mind for me was when Oakland, California, residents turned the incident with BBQ Becky into one big "BBQing While Black" cookout the next weekend. The African roots of Blackness account for why Black women, men, and children through the years have—as a whole—accomplished the psychological fortitude that keeps us going. You can access this fortitude by investing your time in community efforts and with those who affirm who you are. Fortitude is about having a firm, unshakable foundation: yes, unfortunate things will happen, but when you know who you are, you can stand amidst the forces that would otherwise take you out.

Reclaiming your mind and who you are must therefore be based in action so it can be something we share with each other—and do together. I once visited Mickey Leland College Preparatory Academy for Young Men here in Houston, Texas, with my son for a Scouting activity. The school is affiliated with an historical site that was originally established for freed Black people. Along the walls are powerful images of Black people and descriptions of their accomplishments. I imagine that the type of learning that takes place in this institution would inspire awe in any of us. We need to feel awed by ourselves.

In the same way that there have been strategic efforts to remove your identity, you must strategically participate in an active and intentional counter-initiative to get back on track. This is for you and for your children, especially if they are not enrolled in a school that is intentionally doing this already. White children see themselves represented in all aspects of life (the good and the bad), and you must be sure that your children are seeing themselves doing more than playing basketball or football, and dancing.

Ways to Make Your Reclaiming Education a Lived Reality

Your objective for your children is to undo the worst experiment to happen to a people ever in the known history of humanity. You may still think of slavery as something that happened a long time ago. The effects are so powerful that you do not realize how powerful they are. Your foremother was violently snatched away from the rest of her family and taken to a foreign place where she knew no one. What she passed on was the best that she knew how to do, but she did it in a community. Undoing this psychological damage will take a person-by-person, family-by-family, and generation-to-generation effort. It has to be done while classrooms are still reducing your family member down to "a slave" or, as cited in some Texas history books, "workers." The level of systemic brainwashing is unbelievable at times.

Your mission is huge should you choose to accept it. If you are the mother of young children, your goal is not for them to be the best people that they can be. Your ultimate goal for them is to recognize that they are part of a larger community of Black people who must eventually come together to raise the well-being of the community and not just their individual selves. The truth is, we cannot be our best possible selves by ourselves.

This is part of the reason that Ada and her family survived even if they were not physically together. They came together with a community to save and protect one another. They did not see themselves as individuals. The reasons that "everyone else can come here and do better than us" is because (1) they came here willingly and (2) they know who they are. African Americans often wonder how other "others," particularly Asian Americans, seem to do so well. Being captured and being forced to relinquish one's identity exacts a toll. You cannot minimize the benefits of being able to work together to survive and maintain a strong sense of cultural identity.

Until things change in our society, you will continue to be in a constant state of either trying to raise your fortitude or holding on to the little piece of psychological fortitude that you have so you can, in turn, uplift the PF of your teenage son or your ten-year-old daughter. Immersing yourself in cultural traditions as a family is an effective way to fortify everyone. Here are some leads to follow as, together, we work to claim a different future.

Gather stories. Use family reunions as opportunities to share stories about your ancestors.

Create traditions. If you do not have a tradition that affirms your Africanness, be creative. Some celebrate Kwanzaa annually beginning on December 26 through New Year's Day. If your family has not previously participated in a Juneteeth festival, it could be a meaningful annual event.

Visit community resources. Take advantage of opportunities that exist in your community. Go to the local African American history museum and other Black cultural institutions. In Houston, we have ample choices for Black cultural enrichment, including the Houston Museum of African American Culture, the African American Archival Library at Gregory Lincoln, the Buffalo Soldier Museum, Project Row Houses, and the University Museum at Texas Southern University. These institutions and their programming hold so many rich and empowering messages about who we are and the traditions of achievement and creativity that got us here, that just walking through one of their doors has the potential of raising your psychological fortitude by a noticeable measure. Most cities offer similar types of culturally immersive experiences. Seek them out in your town.

Take culture vacations. Plan your family vacations around visiting cultural experiences in other parts of the country. The National Museum of African American Culture and History in Washington, DC, is an excellent family destination. When you visit the National Museum, if you can, avoid going on a holiday so that you can truly sit with the experience. Spend time on the bottom floors, which are devoted to our historical journey to freedom from the Middle Passage up to the present. Notice the details that you knew but also recognize the strength of those people. That strength is in you. Recognize that strength in you that is your responsibility to use to help Black people.

Actively join groups that speak to Black interests. It annoys me when white people get upset about us having our own organizations and clubs. They have no idea what it is like to be misrepresented or outright ignored, bombarded with messages that we do not belong, and devalued as lesser than someone of European ancestry. You must be unapologetically active in connecting with people and with experiences that will affirm you. Doing so raises your psychological fortitude.

Curate influences at home. Being at home with little ones means that you might find ways to incorporate images of Black people in their early socialization. Buy Black dolls with natural hair. If they do not exist at your favorite store, buy one on Etsy. Make sure that you have Black History Flashcards available to practice learning about accomplishments that served to advance our society. In the presence of your children, be conscious of the way in which you talk about Black people in your family and in the media. If you allow your little ones to consume mainstream television, counter the negative and incorrect narratives about Black culture and behavior.

Be selective about your TV shows. The ignorance that women are exposed to when they see Black women fighting on television is not conducive to well-being. Such programming is demeaning. It is bad enough that non-Black people are entertained by how we mistreat each other. It is even worse when we are entertained by and participate in it. To paraphrase Carter G. Woodson, "If you can control a woman's thinking, you do not have to worry about her actions." By now, I hope, you are beginning to think differently about who you are. You see the need to take a more intentional route to improving your PF and protecting that of your young son and daughter. They have to use their critical thinking skills to recognize Black empowerment versus efforts to undermine Black people. If there are no inspiring television shows available that you can relate to, maybe you will create one. No vision is too big.

Dream bigger than the American Dream. Write your own future—one that does not hinge on how much of a white middle-class reality you can create for your daughter. It might somehow seem the easier route, but only because that route will encounter the least amount of resistance from the oppressor and those who are oppressed in the mind. Suicide occurs when there is no hope for the future. You can no longer be reactive to everyday discrimination and subtle messages that your voice and your existence are valueless. "America" will find ways to be what it has always been, so stop waiting for goodness to prevail. What if goodness is waiting for you to use your gifts to lift your own self up? Celebrate who you are rather than mourn fearful women who will call the police on you. Under no circumstances can you reclaim your mind and obtain peak fortitude without embracing who you are or who you are to become.

Using Cultural Protections Wisely

I do not have all of the answers, but I know that you have to continue to tap into your creativity to accomplish what you were put on Earth to do. You stand on too many shoulders to deny what your ancestors bring to the table. The same forces that propelled Shirley Chisholm, Maya Angelou, and Katherine Johnson are in you. Your ancestors used the worst parts of the pig to create meals that some now call delicacies. Those foods fed the hungry and saved lives. I am not advocating for you to embrace chitterlings. My momma said you can't eat from everybody. Instead, I am advising that you be willing to think outside of the box to create and pull from your culture what you need to thrive.

As a final caveat, connecting yourself and your family to your African cultural identity is not a substitute for getting treatment for your trauma symptoms, your severe worry, or your depression-induced sleep problems. It could help in the short term, but meaningful relief from these types of problems will be helped with very specific kinds of therapeutic intervention. Tapping into your cultural identity is more like using sunblock to block harmful sunrays. If you have a skin cancer, putting on sunblock is not going to fix it. The problem must first be eradicated. Then you can proceed to use protection from that which can do harm. Take care of your serious problems first. Reclaiming your mind requires that you first prioritize taking the necessary steps to address these most pressing issues and then you can proceed to cultivate your cultural protections.

CHAPTER 8

Making the Most of Your Spiritual Resourcefulness

Like me, you probably grew up in the church. As a child, you spent more time there than you would have liked, not knowing that you were learning cultural traditions that are connected to your Africanness—traditions that don't just connect you to another "pew member" at church but also to a larger community. We have traditions like fervent respect for elders, "call and response," and the importance of putting faith in a Power greater than yourself. Traditions reinforce your identity and boost your psychological fortitude.

Though some traditions are fading, a lot of your understanding about who you are and who Black people are began in the Black church. As children, my younger sister and I went to Sunday school, sang in the choir, and were present for at least one night of revival each year when guest pastors preached a sermon. When we went to the church that my mom grew up in, we did not get home until the sun was going down. As a high school student, I was secretary of our church's Baptist Training Union (BTU) that met on third-Sunday afternoons. Church was where I first practiced speaking in front of an audience. I learned a lot in church, but I did not really understand what church meant to me until heartbreak hit during my first year of graduate school.

The relationship that sidetracked me was long distance after we graduated college. He was part of my family, and I was part of his, until he called to say that he met someone else. I was so heartbroken that I failed all my midterm exams. That was not a good look for the only Black person in my PhD cohort.

My aunt suggested that God was trying to get my attention. I could have thought of other ways to get my attention for sure. Life felt so unnecessarily cruel. I called my grandmother to pray for me. It took time, but the only way that I was able to get through the painful end of that relationship was church and prayer. I was in Sunday school class one morning when something the teacher said clicked for me: "Ecclesiastes 3:1, to everything, there is a season…" There is a time and place for all things. For me, that time included the ending of my relationship. Surely, I had heard or read the scripture before, but it was as if I was hearing it for the first time. The scripture helped me move my emotional healing along more expeditiously. It was not the season for that relationship. You may have had struggles in life that compelled you to your own Bible lessons.

Church in Your Time of Crisis

Since I have spent most of my life in Black Baptist churches, I am most comfortable in that tradition. As a result, I talk about religiosity and spirituality from a Protestant-Christian perspective. It is possible that you subscribe to a different faith. You may refer to your God by Allah or as Olodumare. Substitute the reference that makes sense to you. Some will disagree, but however you connect to the Divine Power is all that matters for your PF.

Over the years, you have likely found that the pastor says just what you need to hear when you need to hear it. The pastor may say things like "all things work together for the good" and "no weapon formed against you shall prosper." In moments of your greatest despair, you heard a message that got you through. You have hit some rocky times in your life, but you have survived, and you are stronger for it.

As someone who endures the highs and lows of Black womanhood, I know that your faith in God has had an impact on how you have managed to sustain the psychological fortitude that you have. Your faith may be the reason that your PF is 40 and not -40. Your belief in a

Power greater than you is also a critical part of what it means to be African.

Even if you do not relate to being African and have only ever seen it as "backwardness" at worst or something to which you could not relate at best, your foremother brought her spirituality with her from West Africa. She went through the most trying of times. Her humanity was denied, but she somehow believed that God and the ancestors would get her through. This powerful spirituality, along with enormous creativity and the instinct to survive, was passed on to you.

Your sense of spirituality didn't show up miraculously in your mother. African people are a spiritual people. Though we may refer to the Spirit by different names, at the core of our beliefs is a faith in that which cannot be seen. The capacity to *know* without *seeing* and to shun atheism isn't just African American. It's African. Even if you do not personally experience the kinds of "burning bush" and parting of the Red Sea miracles that are described in the Bible, you know that there are wonderful things that have happened in your life that were not of your own doing. There are also situations that could have happened from which you were spared. All of which are attributed to the grace of a Power that is higher than you.

What Spirituality Contributes to Your Life

Spirituality and religiosity are part of what it means to be Black. It is not by chance that 78 percent of African Americans are Protestant compared to only half of all adults in the United States. Only 1 percent of African Americans claim to be atheist or agnostic.[34] I suspect that this 1 percent are also more likely than other Black folks to see themselves as "just American" and not as people whose identity and culture are rooted in an African heritage. Those individuals do not connect with what it means to be Black.

Even if you are a "CME," a Christian who goes to church only on Christmas, Mother's Day, and Easter—and you cuss sometimes (or all the time)—you know that there is a God. Even if your prayer life has faltered, it did not fall completely by the wayside. Religion gives you structure and organization so you know where to go, when, and what to do when you arrive. Some experts think of religiosity as how we use our belief in a Higher Power to act, like going to church and praying. Spirituality is how you choose to live a life of faith even if you are not religious.

Dr. Jacqueline Mattis is an expert in African American and Afri-Caribbean religiosity and spirituality at the University of Michigan. She talks about spirituality as a relationship but also a "journey of self-reflection, self-criticism, and self-awareness that culminates in a greater understanding of the relationship between self, God, and the larger community (including the community of ancestors)."[35] She acknowledges the individual belief in and connection to metaphysical forces, including God and ancestral spirits. I especially like this capacity to be so aware that you can connect to a deep power within you that is also in sync with a Higher Power. At the core of your African-centered culture is spirituality. The opposite is materialism or an emphasis on what you have and can acquire. It is okay to want that Range Rover. I am claiming one for myself one day. However, having peace in yourself, including a sense of who you are as a woman of African ancestry, is what truly matters.

I recently picked up a copy of Susan Taylor's *In the Spirit*. Ms. Taylor is an esteemed former editor of *Essence* magazine. In one essay, she talked about being down on her luck and ending up in a church after she sought care in an emergency department for what she thought was a heart attack. Once they confirmed that she was medically okay, she walked home from Manhattan to the Bronx because she could not afford a taxi. While walking, she happened upon a church and felt drawn in for no reason that she could explain.

The sermon that she heard changed her life. In what was one of her darkest hours, she was able to hear a message that shifted her life course. For some, church or another religious setting is the easiest place to connect with a Higher Power. There are no perfect churches, but it would seem unwise to let your search for the perfect place of worship keep you from getting to your next level.

In Black churches, you can be happy and cry, and feel something deep in your soul and not know why. Black folks who struggle all week need a Word from the Lord. So you can get on a path that will help you connect to a Higher Power, you may want to find a place that you can go to at least to get your rhythm going.

If you are an introverted person who does not like people in general, you are going to have to work smarter than the extroverts that you have encountered. You have to be strategic about how you use your people-energy, but that does not mean that you sit at home. Because Black churches are everywhere, you can locate one that you might like and eventually join one of the lower-key committees. If you visit a church that does not feel quite right, visit another one.

Pray for Guidance on What You Can Do for You

When you go to church, why not pray for faith that God will give you guidance for what you need to do? You might ask God to put someone in your life who will help you meet your life goals. You might ask for God to make your path plain.

You might go to church in a fog with no expectations from the church service. The pastor is preaching, and you do not feel a thing. At least half of those around you are excited about the message, but it is not connecting for you. I go to a church where the congregation is sometimes projected on the wall between showing whoever is in the pulpit or the singing choir. More often than not, I see disconnected faces even when the preacher is sharing the "good news." Consider what your face would say if it were projected back at you during a religious service. If your arms are folded and you're not inspired or moved on most Sundays, you may want to identify the distraction and work through it or find another church. If you are not gaining motivation or learning ways to be a better you, find another church.

You are worried, though the Bible says be anxious for nothing (Phil. 4:6). You are sleepy, because you average five and a half hours of sleep on most nights. Perhaps the roadblock is something else. You enjoy hearing the choir sing, but you are missing out if you are not able to benefit from the message that is struggling to get through to you. That is why you feel better during the church service for a little while, but your mood slumps by the time you get to the parking lot. By the time you get to the grocery store to get what you need for dinner, you're already in a bad mood. You may need to jot down one note from the day's sermon. Just one note or reminder of the Sunday message can get you through a few more days.

Religion Comforts You—Spirituality Grows You

A few years ago, a producer for Bishop T. D. Jakes's talk show contacted me to be the show's guest expert psychologist. Bishop Jakes is a well-known African American pastor who has sold millions of inspiring books and developed popular movies. The topic for his talk show on the day that I was to contribute was mental health. I almost declined the offer, in part because I was afraid. My excuse was that I would not be able to coordinate my life in time to fly to Los Angeles for the taping. Fortunately for me, a very wise colleague convinced me to go.

Before that occasion, I had only participated in local television, so I had some nerves about the national television appearance. To my credit, I answered Bishop Jakes's questions, flawlessly. When everything was done, one of the show's producers said, "People are going to be looking for you." I never think much of what I do, but I was convinced by her words. By the time I returned to Houston, my anxiety was at 85, with 100 being the highest level of anxiety that I could imagine.

I was safe and sound and had done my part to contribute to an important conversation on mental health, but a little voice was telling me that I had a lot more work to do. I told that little voice that I would not and could not, and that there was surely someone more capable and more knowledgeable. I recall being in church shaking, literally. In my heart, I felt that I was supposed to be doing more for my community— using larger platforms to talk about suicide and emotional well-being. But I was afraid and shaking with fear. Who was I to think big? I was so anxious that I did not even bother praying about it. I just wanted the bizarre shaking to stop.

You have likely been in a situation or two that you tried to think or will your way out of. Praying never even entered your mind. You just wanted the thing to go away and figured that it would on its own. Just give it enough time, and it will pass. For me, Spirit was not going to let it go. Instead, the pastor preached about Joshua, who did not feel prepared to lead the people as he was ordered to do. Despite his fear, Joshua was assured that God would not leave him or fail him and that he was to be strong and courageous and not tremble. The message for the day was just what I needed to hear. I was feeling more confident by the end of the service and ready to get to work on the next steps for fulfilling my life purpose.

How You Use Religion and Spirituality Can Cause Problems

Despite your faith in God, it could be inadvertently hindering you from achieving optimal psychological fortitude. Consider this: Do you think that your God wants for you to be miserable? Being spiritual does not mean suffering with severe depression. How can you go to church Sunday after Sunday, waiting for something to change, when you have done nothing yourself? What's keeping you from relocating to a new city, changing careers, getting to work on the business that has been on your heart for four years, or seeing a therapist?

If you have been saying that you are "waiting on the Lord," it is possible that the Lord is waiting on *you*. You must hear the preacher's message and *apply* the text to your life. Don't hear or read the Word and stop there. You insist on staying in your miserable, but familiar, job to wait on the Lord, but your waiting could be a crutch. You need to have a mind-set to act on behalf of your own well-being.

Imagine that your younger sister is making good money but is miserable at work. Meanwhile, she has an idea to start a school in her community that will serve the needs of Black children. If you can encourage your sister to pursue her passion, can you also encourage yourself along the way? If you completed your self-assessment and have concluded that change is necessary for your psychological fortitude, you can ask God to "work it out" and put a strategy and plan in your heart for a new direction in your life.

Staying the Same Is Not a Forever Option

Recently, my pastor preached something that synced wonderfully with my thinking about church as group therapy (though with less of the sharing among group members except to say "Amen"). In group therapy, there is a group of similarly troubled individuals who meet weekly or twice each week with a facilitator who teaches some skills, but generally guides the group to insights that allow them to feel better or gain some hope about their future circumstances.

Whether you attend a religious service weekly, only in times of most distress, or somewhere in between, the religious service is like a group therapy for you. You generally gain some sense of hope that God will make a way. Maybe you feel empowered to withstand your enemies. In any case, my pastor recently made a good point about this. We need to go to church to change. We don't need church to *feel* better but otherwise remain the same—same thoughts, same behavior, and same outcome. Something about how you think and what you do needs to fundamentally change as a result of your Sunday or Wednesday night participation. This is how you raise your PF.

Spirit is the little voice that you ignore on most occasions because it is taking you out of your comfort zone, because it seems ridiculous, or because you rather overthink things. If your thoughts are riddled with fear or tainted with depression, they are useless thoughts. I have been working on listening to my own little voice (that I know is my unfiltered spirit) for little things, like going back in the house to get the lotion that I don't think I need but do. My expectation is that the little voice will show up even more for the big things if I listen for the smaller things.

Maybe you have had much more than your share of bad things happening in your life. This may be evidence that you are off course and need to go in a different direction or take a different path. However, between your anxiety or depression and your determination to "wait on God," you remain stuck. The amount of time in which you remain stuck is up to you to decide. Even if you go to church regularly, something in you is supposed to be changing. What if you used what you learned on Sunday morning to change you rather than to endure?

Cultivate Active, Not Passive, Faith

If your psychological fortitude is forever teetering on 50 and below, you need to step up your game. There is a biblical scripture that says, "Faith without works is dead" (James 2:17). You may need to pray every day and also work on a step-by-step plan for yourself. Then, put your plan in motion or problem solve what is keeping you from putting your plan in motion.

If you know that your prayer life is on point, but prayer does not seem to be working, maybe your Higher Power is waiting for you to do something different. If your faith leader or pastor or whoever tells you that you do not need any type of therapy, you may want to gather your things and politely excuse yourself from the conversation. I am sure that faith leaders have the best intentions for you. Each person who tells you to pray about a problem is sincere. It is true that prayer changes things. However, I am not sure what the concern is with getting help from a trained professional when you have low psychological fortitude or a serious problem.

Too many members of the clergy subscribe to the idea that you can skip the middleman or middlewoman when it comes to your psychological well-being, though you would not dare do so when it comes to your physical health. You are advised to see a doctor for a lump in your breast, chest pains, high blood pressure, or cholesterol. For your mind, you go to the Lord in prayer. But sometimes God sends a psychologist. Pray for one who either gets their wisdom from a Higher Power or can help you leverage your own spiritual gifts to achieve higher PF.

Even a Faithful Mind Can Go Astray

In my opinion, the topic that is the most risky in Black church pulpits is depression (not tithing). I get nervous whenever mental health or suicide come up. If you visit your church one Sunday looking for encouragement, this may be precisely the day that the pastor seems to be talking to you. Somehow, the pastor knows you are so depressed that you "almost didn't make it here today," but insists that you "don't have to be depressed." At least the pastor has acknowledged that depression is a thing. When the script gets flipped is when you go home and you still feel so depressed that you want to die. Meanwhile, you are feeling lost and disconnected.

After all, the pastor said that you do not have to be depressed, so if you are, something must be wrong with you. You conclude that the depression is your fault or something that is only in your head (and no one else's). This is surely not the intended message, but I see how it can come to that. Though the pastor seems to have a direct connection to your Higher Power, they might not be connected to your individual pain on that particular day. They cannot understand that you are in so much pain that you want to end it all. Your pastor does not intend to suggest that there is something wrong with you if you are thinking about suicide.

You have done an amazing job at hiding your pain. No one really knows. If the pastor knew your pain, their responsibility is to pray. They might tell you about Elijah, a strong man of God who had performed miracles according to biblical scriptures. You may not have realized that Elijah had a run-in with depression in 1 Kings despite all of his accomplishments. However, Elijah was so depressed that he called on God to let him die. Unless the pastor is trained in mental health service, they may tell you Elijah's story but have limited tools to help you with your pain long term. You will feel better for a short while, but the pain that drove you to church may take more than a Sunday morning service. It may take working with a professional.

You may have missed an important aspect of the pastor's message that is worth considering. Many pastors are wonderful orators because they know how to connect with people. Notice this: "people." More than one person. The pastor may seem to be speaking directly to you and only you, but you are not the only one in the church who is feeling down and isolated. You are not the first. You are by far the last. Even the pastor in the pulpit has felt depressed and isolated.

Though everyone around you seems to be enjoying a grand life, it is not true. Like you, the woman sitting in front of you is struggling with difficulties in her marriage or with wanting to be married, with her children or not being able to conceive a child, with her job or being jobless, and overwhelming fatigue that has her desperately wondering when and how it will end. You are less alone in your suffering than you know. Perhaps this insight can give you inspiration to press on. You may feel alone, but you are not alone.

In the biblical story of Elijah, he was revived in part because an angel told him to get up and eat. The angel directed him to get moving. Depression can make it hard for you to get moving, but you only need to put one foot in front of the other. Get out of what we call ruminative thinking—when you get in your head and replay your negative self-talk script, the one that says you cannot do, change, have, achieve, or enjoy anything. If you have a favorite gospel song, sing that or read David's songs and poems (Pss. 23, 34, 121) in your Bible app or read about where he encouraged himself (1 Sam. 30:6).

Talking to the Pastor Is Not Getting Mental Health Care

Some years ago, one of my (now-former) pastors called me at my office. In the weeks preceding, several congregants had contacted him with challenges that he suspected could be helped by a mental health professional. He was seeking guidance from me for how to distinguish the kinds of work that mental health professionals do compared to what he does when counseling his church members.

If more pastors would stand up and say that some problems could be helped via a mental health professional, Black folks would be better off. Yes, God can do all things, but we have hospitals nonetheless. There's a story in the Bible that Jesus fed five thousand people with bread, but the pastors who preach that sermon still go to brunch on occasion or wait for someone to cook Sunday dinner.

You see where I am going with this. Stop acting as if "supplying all of your needs" (Phil. 4:19) is why you do not go see a professional. The church is not why you fear telling all of your business. Indeed, all that you have to do is "take it to the Lord in prayer," but you can take your need for a professional to the Lord.[36] If you are real about it, it's not that the church is the primary culprit for your limiting beliefs about therapy.

As my momma used to say to us as kids, you "hear what you want to hear." In some churches, I do think that the clergy discourage mental health expertise, but the reality is that you use religious doctrine to support your fear of talking to a stranger. Perhaps God spoke to Moses through a burning bush because there was no other means to reach him and no cell phone service. We have made progress. Use it.

In the same way that your mother and grandmother relied on faith as Black women, you have also. You may have even gone to your pastor for counseling. If you are lucky, you have access to clergy who are trained in mental health. They are more likely employed at larger churches. If you are at a smaller church, you rely on the pastor.

I am not saying that this is bad. Some pastors are psychologically savvy, but very few are mental health professionals. Your pastor can counsel you on how you are on the wrong path and how you can pray and fast to deal with your distress. Your pastor may challenge you not to "lean unto your own understanding" (Prov. 3:5) despite how intelligent and upwardly mobile you are. This is all very important. However, if you are to get out from under crippling anxiety, there are tools for that. If you are exhausted but do not sleep at night because you keep waking up with stuff on your mind and cannot go back to sleep, there is help for that. There are a number of therapeutic interventions for which your pastor, if not trained, is unaware.

You Are the Master of Your Peace

Having access to a Higher Power is important because you are not going to be able to *survive* everything that comes at you without a strong dose of spirituality. This must be a spirituality that you can access. In that moment when your little one will not go to sleep or will not stop whining, you must be able to still the thoughts that say you are about to lose your mind. You must know who and what to call on and what to do to access your strength and self-discipline to hold on (Pss. 121:2, 46:1).

In that moment of lowest fortitude, one thought that will get you through is "trouble don't last always." You may have heard this assertion from time to time on Sunday mornings in part because the struggle for your sanity is an ongoing fight. It is a fight for each moment and each second of your happiness. Think of your psychological fortitude especially in those moments of greatest challenge. You have to make a decision that your happiness is yours as long as you claim it. You cannot relinquish control of your life and cultural strengths, idly raising your children to fit into white middle-class America and hope they will be okay. You can go this route, but you may be adding unforeseen problems to their future selves.

Instead, spend time deciding what would be important to you if you were not trying to fit a square peg into a round hole. Seek spiritual discernment through prayer and meditation. Discernment requires focus, but it is a tuning in to your own spirit that strengthens as you use it.

You will need to access your spirit-self to overcome those unhelpful thoughts that your situation and future are hopeless. Just when you think you have your financial situation figured out, a new curveball strikes, and your car's transmission goes out to the tune of $2,200. Just when you think that your son's behavior challenges are over, you get a call from the assistant principal at his school. You wonder how your spouse can be so selfish when you too work full time and then come home and work your second job as Mom. It's not fair.

In chapter 11, we will talk about how you think about people and situations around you. You will need to be able to ground yourself and resist problematic thoughts because they will keep coming until you figure out how to manage them or work with a therapist to help you manage them. If your favorite gospel song does not work, recite your favorite scripture. You do not have to make a huge shift overnight. If you are like me, picking up the Bible and reading a random chapter is unlikely to work. If you have a specific book and chapter in mind, that would be more helpful to you. Here are some specific steps that you can take to get your spiritual mind in gear:

- Consider a time that you feel most at peace and least troubled. Go "there" as often as you can. Are you sitting outside or inside? Is there silence? Is it early morning or just before bedtime when you feel this peace? Take advantage of that time. Recreate it whenever you can.

- Search in your biblical app for "what the Bible says" about your specific struggle. My app highlights what the Bible says about "hope," "strength," "forgiveness," and "fear," to name a few. You can also search for scriptures online. When you take notes in your religious service, organize them under topics that you may need to return to in the future rather than in chronological order. In my electronic notes, I include keywords so I can search for them at a later time.

- Make a list of your favorite scriptures for "when I feel lonely" or "when I need encouragement" or whatever you feel you need most often. After a while, the scripture will become ingrained in your memory.

- To help build your scriptural memory, post encouraging scripture on your bathroom mirror. Your sticky notes can help restructure your unhelpful thoughts. Rather than replaying in your head all the ways that your supervisor annoys you, try "the Lord will fight for me and I will hold my peace" (Exod. 14:14). Get through your day with this scripture in mind rather than have your supervisor in control of your mind. Getting angry is understandable, but what you *do* with your emotions puts you back in the driver's seat.

- If the Bible confuses you or puts you to sleep, find a self-help book that allows you to make sense of biblical lessons. Keep the Bible nearby for when you have trouble falling asleep but need a "screen-free" source of inspiration.

Biblical Scriptures as Therapy

One of things that intrigues me about Bible scriptures is how well they line up with psychological interventions. Again, I reference the Bible because it is the religious text with which I am most familiar. My psychological approach, on the other hand, is centered in cognitive therapy and changing how you see or interpret situations in order to better manage them. Two different people can experience the same event and walk away with different interpretations. As an example, my husband has a habit of doing things without getting my input. I prefer that he ask me about situations that could involve me. Instead, he is thinking that he is not bothering me, while I'm thinking that he doesn't care about my preferences. Over the years, I have worked hard to remind myself that he does not mean any harm and that there is likely a reason (at least to him) for what he does. When I forget to tell myself this, I stew over how he could have just talked to me.

Change can be an ongoing process. Old-school pastors say that "God is a mind regulator" and cite scripture that says you can be "transformed by the renewing of your mind" (Rom. 12:2). Biblical writers insist that you cannot accomplish anything without your mind intact. This would seem to be an important principle in cognitive therapy.

As another psychological fortitude tool, you can identify gospel songs that are particularly moving to you. When you get off from a long day of work and anticipate getting dinner together while navigating homework that you half-understand, it could be a good boost to your fortitude to play your favorite song before you get out of the car. A song is less than five minutes. You can do that for yourself to get your mind right. Dr. James Jones, distinguished professor emeritus at the University of Delaware, talked about rhythm, a certain pattern of movement and flow, as integral to our cultural heritage. He suggested that music and dance are an expression of our own internal rhythm. This importance of music, dance, rhythm, and flow are probably not surprising to you. Feel free to add creativity and hustle to the mix. None of it is random to our culture.

When you find yourself particularly disconnected and "off," music may be able to bring you to where you need to be. There are two things you can do that would be easy:

- Create a playlist of your favorite gospel songs. One of my all-time favorites is old-school: "That's When You Bless Me" by the LA Mass Choir and Avery Sunshine's performance of "Safe in His Arms" always stop me in my tracks. You might include a traditional hymn, such as "I Need Thee Every Hour" or "Never Would Have Made It" with Le'Andria Johnson for something more contemporary. When things aren't going your way, "I Won't Complain" by Rev. Paul Jones, "Grateful" by Hezekiah Walker, or any gospel song performed by Fantasia Barrino are all good options.

- If you do not use Spotify, learn how or simply save your songs in your YouTube for easy access. Whatever you need to do to maintain an accessible playlist will be well worth the effort to reset your mood when things aren't going your way.

Your Spirit Is Like Your Phone-a-Friend

Do you remember the show *Who Wants to Be a Millionaire?* It was a trivia show whereby contestants answered increasingly difficult multiple-choice trivia questions. With each correct answer, the contestant inched closer to the million-dollar prize. To make things interesting, each contestant was given "lifelines" to help get to the next level of the competition. One lifeline was to phone a friend.

The contestant could have prearranged friends in the cue to call and discuss the possible answer for thirty seconds. At the appropriate time, the contestant would tell the show producers which friend to call.

Sometimes, the friend would say, "I'm sorry, I don't know," and that was the end of the call. On other occasions, the friend would give an answer and say that they were certain of its accuracy. The contestant would give that answer, the audience and I would cheer, and the contestant would move on to the next round.

There is so much awesomeness in this phone-a-friend game show that is a metaphor for your life. When you need some answers, you have to know who you can talk to and who you would rather not. Whenever I watched *Millionaire*, the friend always answered. I assume that they knew to be on standby. These days, friends may be too busy to respond. Yet, you are connected to a Higher Power that is the best phone-a-friend ever.

You are connected to a Spirit that is always available and will always guide you in the right direction as long as you take time to call. Maybe your spiritual phone-a-friend is blocked by everything that you have going on in your life such that you never take time to sit and be introspective. Maybe your spiritual phone-a-friend is blocked by social media as you constantly check to see what everyone else is doing and wearing and consumed by. The Bible is surely one of the most boring cover-to-cover best sellers to ever hit the stands, but it is a best seller for a reason. To begin your spiritual practice, you do not have to start with the King James Bible. Perhaps you could use a different version. Begin wherever makes sense. You may have to talk to God or quietly meditate so God can talk to you whenever you need to phone a friend.

Religion, and, perhaps more importantly, your faith, has given you hope in tough times as well as reassurance that you are not alone. You know that there is a Higher Power and that you alone are not responsible for everything that happens to you and for you. Because of this, you make sense of things that may not otherwise make sense. For the most part, your life has meaning even if you are not quite on your path. Unfortunately, the church has had a dual role as both a source of strength and, if you let it, a barrier to your PF. Find a place that will be a source of strength if you are not already there.

Our culture of resilience may have inadvertently contributed to a culture of masking psychological problems. You have done such a good job that you may have lost contact with your inner self and spirit. It is one thing to survive the unreasonable expectations that have been put upon you from the time that you started kindergarten until now. It is another thing to revisit your inner mind and the authentic you so you might live a more fulfilling life. This is how you will access the dimension of yourself that allows you to thrive and to accomplish the unimaginable.

Are you familiar with the author Audre Lorde? She is a superbly inspirational writer. One of my favorite quotes of hers is "Caring for myself is not self-indulgence, it is self-preservation, and that is an act of political warfare."[37] Maintaining your mind will take aggressive strategizing against rivals who would otherwise continue to keep your sanity from you. "Hope," as in "I hope things get better," will never be a strategy. One of the ways that you care for yourself is connecting with your spirit. Stop doing the things that everyone is expecting of you so you can nurture the real you.

Church, Like You, Can't Do It All

The church will always be a resource, but it is time for you to get to another level. I do not believe that your passive overreliance on Sunday church service is the only barrier to amplifying your psychological fortitude. You buy into a culture of doing things on your own and without any type of help so you can be a strong Black woman. When popular entertainers, such as Gabrielle Union, talk freely about seeing a therapist, those disclosures inspire conversations in a culture that has historically seen therapy as another "white thing." Fortunately, therapy is becoming less of a white thing.

If the church reinforces your beliefs and fears about getting help from a professional, try instead to pray, listen, and apply what you have learned about your PF. If your PF has been so low that you have considered suicide, see a professional. If you watch church on your iPad because you cannot leave your apartment or feel uncomfortable around people, there is help for that. If you have chronic struggles, have fasted and prayed, and feel that your life is going nowhere, it might not hurt to see a professional who can help you incorporate prayer into a new direction for your life. I am not discouraging you from asking the pastor for prayer and counsel, but that cannot be *all* you do.

I do not have all of the answers for your life figured out, but I know a few things for sure. I doubt that you went to your pastor for a flu vaccine. If what you have been doing is not working, you have a formidable task ahead of you. The good news is that you only have to tackle it minute by minute and day by day. Even when you find yourself in a space of feeling like you just cannot go on, you can because trouble does not last always (Pss. 30:5). Whatever it takes for you to tap into that God, the Power, that Spirit, the thing that makes you special as a Black woman, the thing that has kept you going up until this point, it will make you great. Because no one is coming to rescue you, it is imperative that you are more intentional about accessing what you have and who you are.

CHAPTER 9

Being Genuine About Needing Help Makes Getting Help Possible

Every single person on Earth needs reinforcements to be successful and to maintain a reasonably healthy lifestyle. Whether you are a CEO of a major corporation, a stay-at-home mom of three, or a graduate student anticipating your first "real job," you need backup from time to time. To borrow a basketball analogy, we sometimes need "assists" to stay on our game—on the job and at home. When a basketball player cannot get to the rim herself, she gets an assist from another player. One player gets credit for the assist. The other player gets credit for making the basket. The efforts of both players are required to score the goal. Codependence among team members is necessary for your best game.

This is also true in life. You may not be able to get all of the laundry done on your own, but if someone does something to assist, you meet your goal, and with your mind intact. Maybe you *can* coordinate the school carnival on your own, but if you have backup, you can enjoy some of the carnival too and maybe save yourself from being physically and emotionally drained in the end. If you ask your spouse but they are unable or unwilling to provide reinforcement to get dinner together for your daughter, it won't hurt for the family to have pizza two (or even three) nights in a row. And do not add to your worry: you will not suddenly stop cooking healthy and nutritious meals altogether.

This is what you do in the name of your psychological fortitude. Ideally, you would benefit from both an honest friend to help you figure out your life as needed and a professional counselor to help you process the challenges of your life. But to start, set the essential goal of having and using allies.

You may need to figure out some things for your child who is struggling with not having friends, but it is just as important to both of you that you figure things out for yourself. Not only have you been doing your best at being a good parent, but you have done such a fantastic job of presenting yourself so well in the world that even you do not know when you could use some reinforcements. As they say in the Black Baptist tradition, you do not look like what you are going through or have been through. Good. But don't let that reality trick you into thinking all is well.

You have lived long enough to know when your son, daughter, or best friend is going through something serious, emotionally. You also know yourself well enough to sense when things are not right with you. Serious psychological problems are often challenging to recognize among Black people when they are just "brewing" and in precrisis mode. This chapter will provide context for why and empower you to determine when you or someone you love needs help with their PF. It can be detrimental to wait for life to get better on its own. Honestly evaluating our circumstances is key for making important lifestyle changes.

Re-Envisioning "Help"

Since we are working on changing the way that we do things, let's reconsider the word "help." We can acknowledge that something (or some things) may need to change and that some type of help is needed when a situation cannot fix itself. Often, however, we believe that "help" means that someone must charge in, take over, or assume responsibility for what is not working. But taking charge is not likely called for and assuming responsibility for someone else's life is not appropriate.

On the receiving end, our notions of "help" also tend to be misinterpreted. When someone offers to help, it seems to suggest that we have a weakness and implies that we cannot handle our problems. You might feel as if there is something wrong with you for needing help.

Because of the fear that "They'll think that I can't handle this," or "So-and-so did it all on her own," you impose unrealistic expectations on yourself that undermine your psychological fortitude. Black women may be most vulnerable to rejecting help. When we internalize demeaning messages about being Black *and* being a woman, we are often driven to "show them" exactly what we can do on our own. I've been there.

We all have low psychological fortitude at times. It shows up even among the people who seem to "have it all." Too often, "having it all," or at least having everything that we need, comes with blinders. When we are not dealing with serious financial, health, or legal issues, other kinds of problems slip through the cracks. Let's talk about it.

Our Children—Hurting but with Nowhere to Go

I once took part in a panel discussion about mental health in the Black community in front of a nice-sized group of mostly Black mothers and their teenaged children. This was not a "down on their luck, barely getting by" Black constituency. BMWs and Range Rovers were sprinkled through the parking lot, and I heard their upper-middle-class statuses in their comments about their children's extracurricular soccer and dance activities. The children in the audience sat with their friends, assuming their "I don't want to be here, but I know how to be respectful" postures. This was sufficient for me. I was a teenager once.

Audience members had been encouraged to submit questions for the panel to discuss anonymously, so, as panelists, we had no idea who wrote them. The event took a serious turn for me when a question was read about "how to help someone who you know is cutting himself." The questioner said he knew for sure that the friend was not taking his prescribed medication (presumably for emotional problems) and that the friend's parents did not know what was going on. I answered the question to the best of my ability, as I knew only what was written on the index card. I advised that the child-author find *someone*, an adult, whom he trusted. It was clear to me that his own parents did not fall into that category, so it would not have been helpful for me to insist on talking to them. This was likely my only opportunity to communicate with the writer. I only knew that the child-author was brave enough to ask for help, even if anonymously. In my kindest voice, I invited the author to talk to me if he was comfortable later in the day. I never heard from him.

It would cause me the greatest sadness if my son were going through something as a teenager and did not feel that he could talk to someone. My ego isn't so big that I think I (or my husband) would be the only acceptable grown-up in which he could confide. I would, most of all, want him to have some mature person whom he could turn to for help.

At the end of the panel discussion event, a young woman pulled me aside. She told me about another child who was essentially contemplating suicide. I wish I could say I was surprised, but I learned the inner workings of adolescent struggles in the mid-2000s when I participated in a suicide prevention training with adolescent girls. At the training, I moderated small group discussions with girls as a trusted adult. The youth were mostly white high school sophomores and juniors who had been selected as peer counselors to provide support to troubled peers. What I learned was that they were themselves dealing with a great deal of depression and drug use, unwanted pregnancy, and very low self-esteem. They were kind, lighthearted girls who talked about their dramas like grown women. They made good peer advisors in part because they had been through a lot in their short lives.

I listened contentedly to the girls until I was "invited" into their conversation. Unless you want an eye roll, it is rarely advisable to prematurely insert yourself into a conversation with teenage girls. Once invited, I attempted to find out if there was any adult in their lives that they trust to talk to. As long as they are talking to a trusted adult (and not just their peers), you can breathe a bit easier. If the trusted adult is you, your responsibility is not to get the child to talk to her parents but to understand her fear about talking to her parents. You could ask questions like:

- "What happened when you tried to talk to your parents about (the issue)?"

- (If she hasn't talked to a parent) "Do you think your parents will be *overly* upset if you tell them what you have been going through?"

- "On a scale from 0 to 10, how angry would they be, with 10 being the most angry that you've ever known them to be?"

- (If anger is 9 or 10) "That is pretty high; what would they *do* at that level?" (Proceed to talk through managing the parents' response.)

- "In a perfect world, what would you want your parents to do?"

As the trusted adult, your goal is to understand her fear and concern and help her walk through getting what she needs from her parent or guardian or maybe even the parent of her parent. If you are not a family member or close friend of the family and she is more comfortable talking to her granny, granny will do. If you can understand what keeps her from talking to one of her direct caregivers, you may be able to offer her a useful perspective to take a chance on opening up to them. Even if they are angry and disappointed, they want the best for their child.

When the counselor pulled me aside at the conclusion of the Black mental health panel discussion to share her concern about a suicide risk, she wanted to consult on whether there were additional steps that she needed to take. The child had already left the venue. When her mother pulled up to pick her up from the event, the girl told the counselor, "You can't say anything to my mom," about the suicide thoughts. Before anything could be done, she skipped off to her mom's car and that was the end of the conversation.

As far as we know, that mom had no idea that her daughter was so disconnected and in such pain. That mom is probably tired and overwhelmed with her own life. She probably has too many meetings to attend. She likely tells her daughter "I love you" every day, and when something seems "off," she tells her daughter, "You know you can talk to me about anything, right?" Maybe the daughter sees how much her mom is struggling and she knows that if she adds another thing, the mom will be overcome with debilitating grief and self-blame, and nothing will have changed in the end. The mom may be secretly concerned that her daughter has the same "issues" that the mother had when she was growing up. To deal with her fears, she tells herself that her daughter has too much going for her to have emotional problems.

Stick to the Truth of What's Happening—Not the Drama

If your son or daughter is cutting themselves or has found another way to do harm to their body, perhaps by hitting themselves and leaving a bruise, you do not have to hit the panic button. You do need to find out what is going on. This "self-harm" has become a common way of dealing with intense emotions among children and adolescents. I am not yet sure what the statistics are for Black girls and boys, but they are as high as one in three for young Hispanic or Latina girls and young women. Increasingly, among preteens and teens, self-harm is seen as typical behavior, though it is *not* healthy by any stretch of the imagination.

Just as is the case with suicide, those who do harm to themselves do not want to die. When they harm themselves, they are doing what they can think of to feel better; in a sense, they are taking control of the emotional pain by inflicting physical pain. If they escalate from managing emotional pain to wanting to die, they are at increased risk for dying by suicide. Being averse to pain is one thing that would typically deter them from suicide. If your daughter hurts herself repeatedly, doing so makes her more comfortable with intense pain and thus less averse to suicide death. Barriers to suicide behavior, such as fear of the possible pain or sadness of how death will hurt the family, are inherent buffers for suicide, so if they do not exist, the risk for a suicide attempt is higher.

Is It Your Teenager, or Could It Be You?

If you are the parent of a child who could be self-harming by cutting her arm or thigh or hitting herself and you are unsure what to do, it is time for some assessment, not just for your child, but also for you. What might keep your child from coming to you with his or her pain? Consider whether:

- your expectations are high, and they do not want to disappoint you

- you only show approval and affection for "good" behavior

- they perceive that you are overburdened as it is and do not want to add to it

- they do not believe that you can help, or worse, that you don't see their problems as a big deal

The best that you can do is to pay attention, be available to listen, and not judge them for what they are going through. Would you talk to someone who you know will judge you? That *no* response goes double for your child.

To help your child, you have to take responsibility for asking questions *and* hearing the answers. You must suspend your prepared response even if you do know all of the right answers. Your goal is *not* to help. Your goal is to find out what is going on. Stop trying to help before you do your best to understand what they are feeling and experiencing. And whatever you do, do not minimize your child's problems. It would be very easy to say, "After everything that I have done for you, you go off and start cutting yourself?" If you perceive that your child's situation is about you, it is time for you to assess yourself.

I know that you are doing your best to provide all that you can for your children. I believe this. I understand that your own family may have been tense and unsupportive. Perhaps you were subjected to high expectations as a child who was overscheduled. But children today are dealing with grown-up issues, and—like it or not—they do not have the resilience to manage what you managed. They are overexposed and underprotected. They are finding out about drugs and sex at much younger ages, but they do not have the emotional maturity or wherewithal to deal with it. (Research suggests that the average male does not have a fully developed brain before age twenty-five years of age.)

Children are getting half of the facts about very complex matters that they do not understand. Your adolescent daughter may seem mature, but she is defenseless. Your second grader needs you to have the where-withal to talk calmly rather than yell at her because your PF is low. If you are on Facebook, consider joining the group "Conscious Parenting for the Culture" to be more mindful of how you interact with your children.

Who Can Best Help Me Help My Child?

Do not wait and hope and pray that things will miraculously get better. If your school-aged child talks about wanting to die or typically has strong emotional reactions to everyday types of problems, it is time to at least talk to a professional for an assessment. Revisit chapter 2, but also pray for direction and find a good therapist or counselor who can help your child get their psychological fortitude up to speed. You can hope that the child grows out of it, but the longer there is a problem, the easier it is to try to "live with it," fold it into the background of life, and keep it moving. Then the problems get worse as time goes on.

I recently assisted a family friend whose seven-year-old daughter was often upset by her little brother's antics. The little brother came into the world thinking that he "ran things." By the time he was three years old, he was a bossy somebody. That meant that the seven-year-old was upset and crying almost daily. She began to have problems sleeping. She was once a straight-A student, but her grades were falling in some classes. Some might see this as a phase. Indeed, it could be. At the point when my family friend contacted me, this very stressful situation had been going on for five months.

This is the thing: if you see a problem, prioritize getting a psychological assessment. Talking to a professional does not mark your child as damaged or mean that there is something wrong with them. It means there is an area of life that needs you to call in reinforcements. Pay attention to "phases" that could signal a more serious problem. Unexplained falling grades are often a clue to a significant problem.

Address it before it gets out of hand so your child does not endure prolonged suffering.

Our Black children are struggling with so much more than what we dealt with as children. Even if your child is growing up in more affluent surroundings than you did, there are new and different dangers. You may be thinking that if you put them with the *right* children or if you live in the *right* neighborhood, your child will be immune to trouble, but that is not true. They are often less likely than you and I were to be surrounded by family and neighbors who care and are invested in their success. Many of us don't even know our neighbors. For Black men and women, navigating workplace politics, buying a home, starting a business, and even venturing to a new vacation spot can feel like a minefield. You can be intentional nevertheless about creating optimal outcomes for yourself and also for your family.

Tips for Finding Psychology Resources for Your Child

Throughout this book, I emphasize finding psychological support from someone whom you can trust and is well trained and in a position to help. I often see clients who say that they received unhelpful services elsewhere. This is not uncommon. I do not work with child client cases, but I do know that professionals sometimes jump in to intervene without knowing what started or is maintaining the child's problems.

Children are less equipped than adults to articulate their frustrations. If you enlist a professional and find that what they are saying about your child is unhelpful, do your best to express your concerns. If they do not seem to understand or are unable to make adjustments, find someone else. You get second opinions for surgery, right? You may not feel that you have time to search earnestly for professional help, or maybe you are looking for an easy out, but I'll tell you, finding a therapist who is helpful is worth it. I talk more in chapter 10 about this, but for children, you might (1) ask your child's pediatrician for referral options or (2) research a "behavioral health" option that is associated with a good clinic or hospital that has a good reputation in the nearest metropolitan area. Certainly if you know someone who is getting care for their child, you can ask them where they go. Some professionals advertise that they work with children and adults. Working with children inherently means that the professional will have to work with the parent or guardian, especially for younger children, but the *expertise* should be in working with children. Because children and adults have very different developmental challenges, I advise that you find someone for your child whose primary expertise is problems that develop in childhood. Even among people who work with children, their expertise will be in different areas, such as ADHD, sleep problems, and anxiety. In sum, well trained mental health professionals will have an area of expertise for which they have clinical experience with children who struggle with the problem.

In Your Own Struggle, If You're Not Doing as Good as You Look, Admit It

You may find yourself crying tears in the bathroom because you are so overwhelmed with things not going your way or because you feel so empty inside. You tell yourself that you have everything going for you, so this must just be a phase. But when you look at your journal, it seems that this phase has been going on for six years or longer. Feeling overwhelmed starts to be your norm, so you tell yourself that it is normal.

This is not normal. It may be the new norm for you and those around you, but it is not okay. If you find that when you let yourself sit quietly for a little while, you can't seem to hold back an overwhelming sense of dread or emptiness, your PF is wilting. You chastise yourself because you feel that you do not have the right to feel empty. You tell yourself that you *should* woman up and carry on. The thing is, what you "should" feel doesn't really matter. It only matters that you are not where you need to be or where you truly want to be.

Keeping yourself busy could be a big part of the problem. It looks so impressive—serving on a time-consuming community board, leading your local Links, Inc. chapter, volunteering for the PTA, and being the primary guardian for your elderly aunt as well as your two middle-school-age children—all while showing up as the most well put-together sista in the room. You do not have the bandwidth to know how you are doing, much less what to do differently. Everything's under control, right? Things will get better once you finish with this one event, or once you figure out how to get out of your current job situation, or once the doctors can give you a proper diagnosis for your aunt's mysterious illness—right?

Meanwhile, you have abdominal pains of your own that you have not seen a doctor to evaluate. You have gained fifteen pounds in the last year. You sleep maybe five hours per night and find that your mind has been going blank more than you can track. Like it or not, your psychological fortitude is low.

As a Black woman, I know that you are one of the best at hiding your pain. You deserve an Oscar and would get one if the Oscars weren't so white and exclusive of Black talent. Our society has forced you to contort yourself in all sorts of ways that are unnatural—just so that you can fit in. You are on your way to becoming a master contortionist. You bend yourself to accomplish superhuman tasks and sometimes manage even to be in three different places at the same time. You don't know when you're coming or going. If this is your reality, start by getting honest about it. This is far from your best life.

Starting to Stop Your Madness

There is a two-part process in all of this for you. The first part is to stop the madness of ignoring your needs. The other part is for you to begin to take steps to actively increase PF. Honestly ask yourself if you have been subjecting your family to the mismanagement of your health. When you are all over the place, exhausted, and hiding depression, are you impatient and snapping at everybody? What are the cascading effects? In the end, are you the mom that you want to be? Are you a mom that your teenagers can come to when they really need emotional support? Have you inadvertently "passed on" your anxiety to your pre-kindergartener who wets the bed? Is everyone on eggshells because they see you repeating old habits that preceded your mild stroke from a year ago?

Perhaps you know better but, for whatever reason, refuse to do better. You could have a health condition that the doctor has told you that if you do not begin to eat right and exercise, you will end up having major surgery. Or maybe you are morbidly obese but seemingly unable to take small steps to increase your healthy physical activities. The question I'm getting at is: Is there a part of you that is waiting to die?

If you are over fifty years old and you have been struggling with the same kinds of challenges all of your adult life, maybe beginning in your childhood, I have the utmost sympathy for you. When you have been struggling with something for that length of time, doing something different now is much harder than if you got help when the problem first began. But this is a message to you if you have a child who is ten, twelve, or sixteen years old who has emotional challenges. Get them help now. Then they won't be in a boat on stormy seas, like you have been, through the decades. Get them a paddle.

Most of us will take major illness for ourselves or our loved ones very seriously. When it comes to our own *mind*, however, we settle for just hoping for the best. It's fascinating. We understand that therapy is for white people. Presumably, pain and suffering are for Black people. I don't know where all we learn this; it seems like it just is.

You figure that you have gotten by thus far without going to therapy and having to tell all of your business, so why start now? You have everything going for you, and everyone around you thinks highly of you. But you know the truth—things are not right. At a minimum, you are not doing as well as you know that you can be doing in your personal life, in your professional life, or in your health. It is time to prioritize your well-being enough to seek a better life for yourself. To do that, you need to see a few things differently—including yourself.

"Sick and Tired" Is a Real Thing

Maybe you don't need help. Maybe you just need to shift course. You work hard and do your best for your family. As you read, you are thinking that everything is not about depression and anxiety; sometimes it's just about fatigue from being stretched too thin. You are Fannie Lou Hamer tired—sick and tired of being sick and tired. You wouldn't be surprised if research eventually found that Black people sometimes die, not of natural causes, but of being *tired*. Being sick and tired can show up in so many different ways. Consider whether either of these sounds like your brand of tired.

Sick and Tired, Brand #1

First and foremost, God is the head of your life—the head but not the tail. Were it not for God, you know that you would have lost your mind a long time ago. This is why you are certain that depression and anxiety have not gotten to you. You go to the adult Sunday school class and Bible study weekly in addition to the early Sunday morning service. Being close to God helps regulate your mind.

In between "regulation," you are in charge of a family that does not begin to appreciate all that you do for them. You have raised three adult children. Only one seems to have done anything for himself, but he moved to the other side of the country and rarely comes home to visit or even calls.

The other two are struggling with their own life situations. Your daughter is a single mom who was really smart as a child but got off track somehow when she went off to college. You never understood what happened, but since she is the youngest, you do everything that you can to help her. Your oldest son has been in and out of jail and on and off drugs. You know his heart. He is a good person but got caught up with the wrong people. He's just like your brother. You wonder when they will get their acts together.

The reality is that they do not have to get their lives on track if they do not want to. You are the lifeline. Just when you think that things are getting better, something pops up. Your doctor tried to put you on a sleep medication, but it made you feel funny, so you don't take it. You know that God will work it all out.

Sick and Tired, Brand #2

Maybe your brand of "sick and tired" comes from being on a job that only pays the bills. It is a good job that pays well and that allowed you to buy your baby Benz, but the work is not anything that you actually enjoy doing. Your coworkers are okay, but you are the only African American woman at the firm. No one else knows the challenges that you have to navigate as a single Black woman. When you're not working overtime, you enjoy hosting big events and decorating, but you are not convinced that you can make a living and maintain your current lifestyle doing what you enjoy.

Your social life is good, though you do not feel as close to your sorors as you would like. Spending time with them is better than sitting at home alone waiting for Mr. Right. As the only one in your family who went off to college, you have never quite fit in with your family. You love being the "favorite auntie" and helping support the family when they need it, but you don't connect with their favorite TV shows or the music that they listen to, and there are too many inside jokes to keep up. It's like you're on the outside looking in with the people who you are supposed to be the most connected to. Your family is proud of your success. You just wish that you did not feel so lonely and isolated. Sometimes you feel like you do not quite fit in anywhere.

At least you are not as bad off as your miserable friend. She is always critical and does not have anything positive to say about anything or anybody. She is so negative that you sometimes avoid being around her. You tell yourself that at least you aren't *that* unhappy. You have survived by telling yourself that no one is truly happy. Some days, you blame social media. Everyone is posting all of their pictures of success, and you feel left out. You don't have anything to post. Your frustration about social media is a powerful reflection that your time to shift is near.

Do either of these hit home for you? Or is there something else that has been bringing you down for years or even decades that you are hoping and wishing and praying will change? In the meantime, you just do your part to get up in the morning, get dressed, and do the same thing over and over again while waiting for the change.

I would like to suggest to you that the change might have to be in you. Unfortunately, you can barely see your way through to the next day. You go on vacation and feel excited to be free of your daily drama (though if you are a magnet for drama, it will likely reach you on your vacation). But then you return to the usual grind. Maybe you haven't allowed yourself to acknowledge how tired you are. Sometimes we just end up in situations without knowing how we got there.

I like the analogy of the frog in the hot pot because it visually speaks to how we unknowingly acclimate to problematic conditions. The frog gradually adapts to each degree of heat. Because the frog does not realize that the heat is turning up, it is eventually cooked. If you are not already, you are at risk for being cooked before you realize it's time to hop. Running around and completely on empty—psychological fortitude at 35 out of 100—you know that there are things that you need to be doing differently, but there are too many people counting on you or you don't have the energy or you just do not see your way out.

Could This Just Be Stress?

One word that I have yet to explore in depth is "stress." You may have tossed that around a lot: "I'm stressed." "I've been under a lot of stress." "My family is stressing me out." "I need to deal with this stress." "I need to release some stress." But what is stress, really? Some would define stress as anything to which the body has to react.[38] It is as simple as that. There is "good stress" and "bad stress." Good stress is helping your sister plan her wedding—the most exciting day of her life. Bad stress is the details that go into planning the wedding. Getting married is great, but the details and the family drama have taken out many a well-intentioned folk. Stress is stress. The thing that is bad about stress is when you get to the point that you cannot manage it and your emotions are overwhelmed. When you do not have the psychological fortitude to deal with ongoing stress for months and years, you have a problem.

This Conversation Is About You—Not Your Representative

This is the thing: We may be talking about two people—you and the persona you maintain in the world. You will have a hard time examining yourself if you cannot give up that persona: that you are the fixer, or that you are the smartest in the room, or that you want everyone to like you, or that you want the promotion. I am telling you what I know.

Some years ago, I was a tenured associate professor. There are multiple levels of advancement in the university system. Not everyone has tenure, and not everyone has the option to earn tenure. I earned tenure in 2010. At the same time, I was promoted from assistant professor to associate professor. The next level was to be promoted to full professor or simply "professor." I was never one to quit, so making full professor was always a goal. You probably have a similar setup at work such that once you achieve some advancement, there is another waiting for you. It's okay because you are a high-achieving go-getter! To earn the rank of full professor, I was told that I would have to obtain a multimillion-dollar grant as the lead investigator. I had been a grant coinvestigator, but never a lead.

I was determined to write a successful grant application. In most cases, one in ten grants is funded, and writing a grant is no joke. Keep in mind also that grants center on area of interest. My area of interest is Black people. As you know, Black people's problems tend not to be a funding priority. I persisted to get the grant because the grant seemed to be the only thing standing between me and the promotion. You have probably had to take this position on occasion, that against all odds, you'd show "them" and every other doubter (including yourself).

In June 2013, I was in my home office and had been sitting in my chair for too long working on the grant. I stood up to get a good stretch, and when I went to sit down, the chair rolled out from under me. I fell and ended up in the hospital. The pain was excruciating. Because I had a preexisting back condition, I needed surgery. Two doctors said that if I did not get the surgery and sneezed the wrong way, I risked permanent paralysis. (I couldn't make this up if I wanted to.) My toddler son had a lot of growing up and running around to do. I had to have the surgery so I would be able to run with him as long as he would want me to. I was unable to submit my grant on time and would have to wait another full year to submit it to the funding agency that gave me the best chance for getting the money. Yet there was an option B. Rather than wait for the next year, I considered option B, a route that had a very short timeline attached to it.

I was stressing myself out so much that I was in a fog. I didn't know up from down. I didn't know whether to continue to push myself full tilt at option A or option B. At some point, option C entered my mind, "What if you don't ever make professor?" I had never considered it before that moment. But I sat with it. What if you never. Make. Professor? I went along and answered the question. It meant that I gave up and that I was a quitter. Not good. It meant that I would be free of chasing something that meant nothing to me—there was a new thought. I got honest with myself: professorship meant very little and wasn't worth the sacrifices that I was making. I was relieved. I was happy. I could make a different decision and go a different route. I was tenured, so I had a job for life as long as I maintained high-quality research, teaching, and service. I was done with chasing the next level. I decided that I would never go up for promotion. I don't remember if I told my husband. I was too content in myself. And I lived my life with option C for as long as that made sense.

In the aftermath of that decision, I saw clearly that people who care about me didn't mind it. Most didn't know any difference. The people who care about you are also not impressed with the discontent you, or the you that tries to impress everybody, or the you that is insecure because you did not finish college, or the you that does not have as many degrees as your sister, or the you that you despise for whatever reason that you have conjured up for yourself.

The Lighter Side of Life

Be willing to let go of who you want people to think you are. Until you do that, you cannot get a good sense of your psychological fortitude. Perfect mom of perfect children, unfazed sister, well-connected soror: keeping up personas can send you to an early grave. You certainly cannot reclaim your mind if you can't have a good giggle at your real and sometimes-pitiful self.

When was the last time that you laughed at yourself? Like really laughed? I laughed at myself today. I was playing Uno with my son and put down a card that didn't match the number or the letter, and I yelled Uno like I won the lottery. My son looked at my card and looked at me, and we had a good laugh at my expense. I told myself yesterday that I would start a new experiment with myself. In the experiment, I laugh whenever I'm frustrated with something. I'm in a bit of a season and need to do some things differently. Sharing this with you, I am more likely to stick with the plan, which includes laughing more, even when it might not make sense to laugh.

How We Fail to Help Those We Love

There are some things we need to own about how our way of doing things enables unhealthy choices in others. I was recently talking with a colleague whose seventy-year-old father passed away two years ago. His father was a diabetic who would pay neighborhood children to pick up pork rinds and diet soda for him at the corner store. He also called his adult nieces to pick up junk food for him. The father did not ever ask my colleague, his son, to pick up forbidden foods, but my colleague knew that this was going on.

I get that it would be hard for you to convince your big mama (or older auntie, or other close relative or friend) to make different kinds of decisions. She has survived some very hard times when Black people were considered even less human than we are now. She might have worked for white people who disrespected her. She might have been forced to ride on the back of a bus. She may have done all of these things willingly to put food on the table and have some sense of self-respect. She may have survived abuse or other mistreatment. Maybe she feels lucky to be alive (or maybe she doesn't). In any case, she is not going to let you or anyone else tell her what she can and cannot eat. If her psychological fortitude is low and she doesn't want to go for a walk even to the mailbox, one of those neighborhood children can get the mail for her. She finally feels like she has earned some respect.

You were probably raised to respect your elders and to not talk back. If she wants a whopper and a shake, you might not question it out loud. That would be disrespectful. Though much is shifting, it is generally not a part of our culture to be disrespectful to our elders. I get it. I was raised in the South in the 1970s and 1980s, so I understand. To disagree with an elder in the family is often unheard of. It does not matter if you are grown and have your own mortgage and car note.

Sometimes my elders do not appreciate when I speak to them plainly about the facts. I have been advised by my own family not to "use that psychology" on them. You do not need a psychology PhD or even a bachelor's degree to use your eyes. If your grandfather or your mother or your sister or your cousin has hypertension or type 2 diabetes, they are very likely on a diet that is supposed to help manage the disease. To not manage the disease is a short road to an early death.

My colleague shared that he knew what his father was doing, but no one said anything. On one occasion, his brother picked up fast food for their father who had just been discharged from the hospital for heart surgery. My colleague left his father at the house with his fast food and without saying anything about it. Saying nothing has probably kept the peace in your own home or in the home that you grew up in. Keeping the peace does not save a life. This is a decision point: you have to decide what is most important. Stop the madness.

Saving a Life and Your Right to Remain Silent

You cannot force your loved one to take self-care steps, but you can support their good decisions and decline to participate in their harmful ones. In the short run, it is so much easier to leave well enough alone. When you are facing a life challenge that you are not ready to confront, the last thing you want is someone sticking their advice and criticism in your business. You don't want them giving you a hard time on top of everything else. If you are struggling with a life-and-death matter, however, even you would want to know that your loved ones are concerned. Try these on:

- "I know you're having a tough time, but it concerns me when you ignore the doctor's discharge plan." *You said what you said. Then, walk away. There is no need for discussion.*

- "I am scared that you will die if you don't try to follow the doctor's recommendations."

- If you see a small amount of effort, encourage it by saying, "I noticed you taking steps to eat better. I'm so glad to see you trying." *Smile and, again, walk away.*

Even if you already know what they are going to say—"It's not about you," "Only God knows the day or the hour"—you are only responsible for supporting their good decisions and not supporting their bad choices. You can do this with honesty and without judgment. This is why you walk away. You are not inviting a discussion. If they want to say something, remain and be respectful. There is no need to argue. They are having a tough time, but you love them. That's why you said what you said.

How Are Your Current Helping Tools Working?

Tools are what you use to help you get out of a stressful or tough emotional situation. Sometimes you get overwhelmed and don't know how overwhelmed you are. It happens whenever you feel that your circumstances are beyond your ability to help yourself or someone else. You just know that you need to go to church (which is a tool) or to call up your sister or a friend or anyone who can help you out of your current bind (another tool). In my work and also as a Black woman, I know that we have powerful tools. But you are probably reading this book because, while your tools have been getting you by, you feel like you are on a roller coaster and can't get off. You need something more sustaining. Maybe your tools don't match the problem. There is, for example, no tool for racism. There is no tool for your brother's drug addiction—at least not for you. Your brother needs his own tools.

You might need to think about how well your tools are holding up. How are your tools helping you with the real problem, or do you need to make some adjustments? I am not suggesting that it does not help you to call your sister. What I am saying is that relying on your sister rather than on your God-given talents or good sense is selling yourself short. Going for a walk to calm your nerves is great. But afterward, walking right back to the same situation that you know in your heart, mind, spirit, and soul that you need to get out of is like sitting on four flat tires. Your. Car. Is. Going. Nowhere. Even if you're pushing it, you are wearing down the rims and causing damage to the tires—some damage you can see and some damage you cannot see. Both types can be irreparable.

Have you ever done that? Isn't that how the body works? We eat too much food or drink ourselves into a stupor. Next thing you know, you've created another problem that you didn't see coming all because your current tools aren't up to the task of your current frustrations.

If your assessment is "something is not working," then begin there. That is fine. What is it that is not working exactly? Break your problem down to the smallest pieces. Let's say you are a workaholic. You cannot enjoy life because you work seventy-hour weeks at a job that you don't even love. You say that you are doing this so you can get the promotion. It is okay to be ambitious, but at what cost? If you are happy and content with the seventy-hour weeks, I am not talking to you. If you are hanging on every word in this chapter, there is a chance that I am talking to you. Only you know.

Make Your Self-Check for Psychological Fortitude a Habit

Recall the psychological fortitude rating system. You can break down psychological fortitude into a measuring system that makes sense for understanding how you are doing. The 0-to-10 rating scale helps get a quick evaluation of yourself without overthinking. It could also help others share their own quick evaluation with you.

Use the rating scale in a way that works for you and the situation. You could ask: How high is your PF now, on a scale of 0 to 10, with 10 being the highest? Or, you could flip the scale and ask: How depressed are you now on a scale of 0 to 10, with 10 being very depressed and 0 being not at all depressed?

You do have to keep in mind what you are measuring and what it means. For PF, you may want to get a sense of how high or good it is, so 10 would feel wonderful. If you're measuring a negative emotion, such as depression, you might ask, "How depressed are you feeling, with 0 being not depressed and 10 being the most depressed you could imagine?" If you think of 0 to 3 as no depression to mild depression, 5 to 6 as moderate depression, and 9 to 10 and highly depressed, your interpretation is opposite of a 10 for PF.

You can easily use the rating with yourself and with others on any topic that you want to quickly evaluate. I use rating scales with doctoral students that I supervise, and I advise them to use it with their clients. I ask students questions like, "How confident are you feeling about your next session?" If they are uncertain, they hesitate. That initial response tells me a lot. Once they give me a number, I know that the number reveals either some of the hesitation or they've gained some new insight into the process of thinking of the rating. Either they are surprised by how confident they are feeling or they are struck by the reality that they are not feeling so confident.

This is the thing about objective numbers rather than subjective feelings like "I'm fine." You may be so good at hiding your feelings from yourself and presenting an illusion that you have bought into your own story. If someone asks you to rate how you're feeling, you have to think about it, especially if the rating does not match what you have been saying about yourself. This looks like habitually saying, "I'm doing good," when in reality, your rating of your fortitude is 4. No ma'am! A 4 is not "doing good." With the rating approach, you can sift through distractions for real information.

You can also use a 0-to-100 scale if you want a broader range or more nuance. But you always have to say what the 0 means and what the 100 means, whether you are talking to your daughter or your best friend. Here's an example: Ask, "On a scale of 0 to 100, how satisfied are you with your life right now, with 0 meaning there is no amount of satisfaction and 100 meaning that you are as satisfied as you can possibly imagine?"

On such a rating scale, you can decide what to do, or you can take it as information. Later, you can talk to your friend and ask, "What's the rating now?" Be careful about your language. You have to be specific. Don't ask, "How high is your rating?" because it sounds like you are looking for a high number. You just want to know, "How would you rate on a scale from 0 to 10 or 0 to 100? What is your level of (satisfaction, joy, sadness, frustration)?" And here is a follow-up: "What would you like that rating to be?"

If the PF rating is at a 5 or lower, you want to do something differently or stop *doing* altogether and take a time-out. If it is at 6 to 7, can you figure out what the roadblock is to getting to an 8 or higher? There is no need to overreact, but also no need to stay where you are. The same is true if PF is on the other end of the spectrum at 3 or lower and especially if it has teetered there for months. This is a problem alert! You want to reevaluate everything about your life. What is going your way, and what isn't? If you are unsure, you may need to call in reinforcements.

Everyone Needs Assists to Get Through Their Game

Shonda Rhimes is one of the most shining examples of Black girl magic of the twenty-first century. Her talents are innumerable. She created

Grey's Anatomy and *Scandal*, a groundbreaking drama that showcased the fictional political fixer Olivia Pope. Because of Shonda Rhimes, we were "gladiators" along with our heroine Olivia for six years. Ms. Rhimes showed us how we could be brilliant and emotional and fearless and vulnerable all at the same complicated time. We could do this while still winning and slaying. This was new imagery for a Black woman that we could relate to. Shonda Rhimes did that.

Despite Ms. Rhimes's inspiring success and creativity, she reveals in her book, *The Year of Yes*, that she struggled with severe, debilitating anxiety. This amazing woman declined coveted talk show interviews due to fear. When she was required to attend events, she sometimes sat silently, relying on fellow guests to fill in the silence. In her book, she described occasions when she was so detached that she did not recall the details of any of these situations. This detachment is not unusual for someone who experiences such severe anxiety. If you have ever experienced severe "stage fright" or panic attacks like the ones that I describe in chapter 4, you know what this is like. Like Ms. Rhimes, you have likely figured out how to avoid anxiety-provoking situations so much so that your avoidance affects your life.

This was Ms. Rhimes's modus operandi until the day her sister made an offhanded comment about the fact that she always said no. Her "no's" were a shield to manage her anxiety. But on the fateful day of her sister's comment, Shonda Rhimes basically turned on her awe-inspiring, superhuman, Black girl magic and proceeded to heal herself of the debilitating anxiety. Who does that? According to the narrative that she detailed in her book, she faced her enormous fears *without* the help of a psychology professional—or, at least, she does not disclose if she spoke to one. But I would not be surprised if she did. If she did not, I am supremely in awe.

To say that I was amazed to read Ms. Rhimes's story would be too small of a word for what she did to change her life. She basically got help—lots of it, in multiple areas of her life. While facing her greatest fears, saying yes to everything, she was fortunate to have the resources to maintain a lot of support around her. Ms. Rhimes shared that when she needed encouragement with personal problems, she called in close friends and family. She has an army of people assisting her at home and at work. At home, she has a supernanny, and at Shondaland, she has all manner of assistants, writers, crew members, and staff. She expressed tremendous gratitude in her book for the woman who helps take care of her children. While you might be shy about your need for help with your little ones, the reality is that we can all use some help sometimes.

Ms. Rhimes armed herself to face her anxiety head-on by calling in reinforcements. She had enough psychological fortitude to take stock and gather her resources, and by doing so, she changed her life. Sometimes what looks like magic is really what happens when a person's will meets her resources. What Ms. Rhimes pulled off, even with her money and connections, was not easy. She was at the height of her success. Like many of us, she was busy, stressed, and pulled in a million directions. To finally deal with and get past her anxiety, she had to decide to make a change, make herself uncomfortable, and commit even when things got hard. You too can make this decision when you are ready.

The Reality Is You Need Reinforcements

Too (too) often, you kick off your shoes, take off your wig, and set yourself in that comfortable pot of water to await the boil. You're cooked before you know it. This probably happens over and over again. It is not your fault. Your psychological fortitude gauge needs realignment. You were doing the best you knew how to take care of everyone, keep up appearances, and not lose your mind in the process. If you are honest with yourself, your psychological fortitude is at 25 out of 100. If anyone asked you for a rating on any given day of how you were doing, you would say "70" when you were secretly knowing "25" and wishing for a "90." The consequence of this dishonesty is that you end up in a space that is hard to recover from but that could have been prevented. The heavy lifting can be challenging, but when you decide to be genuine about your pain, using tools to help you achieve a higher PF becomes possible.

If you ever experienced cramping, headaches, or any pain that you could predict, I imagine that you took ibuprofen or something so the pain wouldn't get so bad that you almost couldn't function. You need to figure out what the ibuprofen is for your psychological fortitude and take it. Is your daughter struggling emotionally and needing to talk to a professional? Are you running around with out-of-control blood sugar and needing to change your eating habits? Have you been thinking that your family would be better off if you were dead? I am here to tell you that you do not have to wait until things get worse. You can do something right now to call in reinforcements.

Now that you know how to honestly assess yourself and why it is important, and now that you have looked at your psychological fortitude and coping tools and determined which are still sharp and effective and which are dulled or broken and no longer useful, you can begin the next steps to improving your quality of life or supporting your loved ones in improving theirs.

CHAPTER 10

How to Make "Therapy" Work, When You Need It

There are psychology professionals who are trained to guide you through your scariest, most debilitating fears so you don't have to be numb, profusely sweating, dizzy, or paralyzed at the idea of talking to a room full of people, flying on an airplane, driving down the street where you experienced a traumatic accident, or even meeting Ms. Oprah Winfrey.

Yes, a therapist can guide you toward your own resources so getting out of bed isn't so hard and purpose can move dread out of your mind. If you are overwhelmed and need help working through some considerable setbacks in your life—the loss of a loved one, a miscarriage, your addiction to painkillers and sleeping pills, your crippling feelings of inferiority, and your recurrent thoughts of driving off the road on your way home after work (and that was just in the last month)—therapy can help resolve the trauma. It can empower you to rise from hopelessness to make beneficial changes in how you live.

When prayer, meditation, churchgoing, journaling, spiritual rituals, and everything else that you tried have been insufficient for you to shake what ails you, you may need professional mental health services or counseling. A professional "collaboration" can help you fix the shortcomings of your current tools (or lack thereof). You may benefit from a shorter-term fix, or you may have a more serious problem on hand.

Unfortunately, the mental health system can be daunting. I aim to help you navigate a complex mental health care system to get what you need for yourself and those you care about. As I mentioned in other chapters, emotional health care is not necessarily designed with Black people in mind. There have been some efforts to be more inclusive of your needs, but there is much more work to be done. You can, nevertheless, benefit from learning tools and strategies that help with common problems that everyone faces.

If you are ready to consider seeking a therapist, psychiatrist, or other mental health professional, I want to remind you from the outset that this is a journey. When you find the right professional to help you make your way to wellness, all the effort is well worth it.

Know When It's Time for Professional Help

If you have Shonda Rhimes–fortitude and resources, you might easily gather your reinforcements when you are ready. But if you do not have that level of resource, you may have to be patient as your change-process begins and shows results. Regardless of who you see, you have to be ready to abandon "business as usual" to increase your psychological fortitude.

Hopefully, you have not waited so long that that you are in crisis. In crisis mode, the goal is to get to a place of feeling stable so you are in control of your life and of your feelings. Once you are out of crisis, you may not be motivated to be in therapy. Instead, you return to the rat race that is your life—the one that drove you to crisis in the first place. Ideally, you seek therapy before crisis so you can learn skills to manage your life rather than continually hoping that things will work out.

Everyone can benefit from a boost in psychological fortitude, including you. You may prefer to ponder what your life would have to look like for you to seriously consider therapy. Will you sustain psychological fortitude of 25 out of 100 indefinitely? Would you stay in your miserable corporate job, holding tight to your creative talents, for five or fifteen more years rather than start your own party-planning business? How long will you wait? This is for you to know in your spirit. There is no reason for you to begin telling yourself that you "should" have started building on your life dream years ago. There is no reason to "should" yourself. That kind of negative self-talk won't help.

You can also be aware that change could include committing to *trying* therapy if you have never done so. You have made excuses for not seeking therapy of any sort because you are so good at just continuing on. Consider this: If you had to relocate after Hurricane Katrina, the most devastating storm that ever impacted the United States, you may be grateful for a fresh start but still be traumatized years later due to devastating loss. There is no expiration date on working through unresolved grief and trauma. I use this example to illustrate how your efforts to persevere despite one or two forms of distress can, over time, become compounded with an ever-growing list of challenges.

Indeed, because you are an intelligent, accomplished individual, you will need to work with someone who can help you generate new approaches and solutions to your problems. You need new tools for your toolkit. Given how much you have accomplished, you can figure out ways to manage your eating that has gotten out of control. If you see a professional, you expect her to have something new to say that you haven't already tried. If all you needed was a new diet, you could figure that out on your own. However, if you have had trouble maintaining the changes that lead to weight loss, that might be a goal to discuss with a professional—especially if your extra twenty pounds (or more) is affecting your health, increasing your risk for heart disease and type 2 diabetes.

If you find that you experience tightness in your chest whenever you have to talk to your boss, that could be anxiety-related panic. If you are not sure that you want to be alive and well, you might consider having a conversation with a professional about your ambivalence toward life because you could be depressed. The truth is, any one of these problems can continue to derail you and keep your psychological fortitude low. Any one of these is enough to justify your decision to seek professional help.

Common Misconceptions About Therapy

There is a common concern in the community that once you tell someone "your business," it will get out. Therapists have an ethical responsibility to confidentiality. If you call a clinic and ask how your sister is doing, they will not provide information about her. They also do not acknowledge whether or not your sister is seeking services. Anyone who is a licensed practitioner has an ethical responsibility to maintain the confidentiality of a client. Even if your therapist happens upon you in public, they would ideally not acknowledge you, especially if you are with other people. It is that important.

Confidentiality requires that your relationship with your therapist remain undisclosed in all possible ways. In the first session with your new therapist, you sign off on an agreement for treatment in which your privacy is a prerequisite of the treatment. The only time that your therapist can disclose to another professional that you are in therapy is with your written consent. In most states, if you are believed to be a danger to yourself or others or to a child or if therapy is court-ordered, then the therapist is mandated to acknowledge that you are in therapy. Even in those cases, however, limited information is provided. Therapists are protective of you and your personal information. If they are not, a complaint can be filed to the state licensing board, citing unethical conduct.

Another common misconception is that you have to be crazy or on the verge of an emotional breakdown to be in therapy. This is not true. You do not have to have a serious problem with depression, anxiety and fear, or alcohol addiction to get help. Given that African Americans are most likely to seek help once problems have become debilitating, you may be at this juncture. Unfortunately, problems are harder to address once they have become serious. I cannot stress this enough. I know that you are doing just fine running back and forth to all of your meetings from the time that you start your day to the time that you pass out at midnight and on the weekends. I know that people are really impressed by you. If you say that you want to shut down the engine to rest and reassess, but are unable to do so, you may benefit from therapy now before the engine gives out on its own.

Finally, therapy is not about being "locked up." Historically, therapy was associated with "insane asylums" where very troubled individuals spent their lives. Indeed, Black people are disproportionately "put away" both in prisons and in long-term mental health facilities. I would be wrong if I did not acknowledge this very real concern. That we represent less than 15 percent of the United States population but closer to 25 percent of those in long-term care suggests that we are overrepresented in mental health facilities. In many ways, these outcomes are a function of (1) misdiagnosis and undertreatment, (2) lack of resources, and (3) delayed efforts to get help. As I mentioned in another chapter, your relative may have met criteria for bipolar disorder when the doctors diagnosed him with schizophrenia and put him on a high dose of risperidone. He was eventually hospitalized because he could not take care of himself and no one else could take care of him. Had he been diagnosed with bipolar disorder and given the appropriate medication, he would have been more likely to have lived a productive life. However, his initial problems persisted, untreated, for so long that the prognosis declined. Timing is important so you receive an accurate diagnosis. This is another reason to seek help before you are in a crisis state.

Begin by Ruling Out Physical Issues

Since symptoms of physical problems and psychological problems can overlap, you want to first address the physical ones because those can have crippling or even deadly consequences. If you have physical health problems or symptoms, including chest pain or even overwhelming fatigue, make sure that you have had a thorough physical examination to rule out physical causes. You also want to make sure that your blood pressure is within normal limits, including in stressful situations. Stroke is a silent killer for African American women who ignore, minimize, and push through physical problems. You cannot be available for the family that relies on you if you are not well. Take care of yourself.

Locating the Right Therapeutic Help

There are many layers and levels to mental health care: Who do you see? How do you go about finding her? I hope to guide you through what you are evaluating as you search for a good fit. Your goal is to find someone who you can trust to keep your secrets (not judge you), hear your concerns, and share ways of gaining some relief from your troubles. I like what NAMI, the National Alliance on Mental Illness, says about the objective for what you are seeking in a therapist: someone who is trustworthy and knowledgeable.[39]

Over the years, I have worked with friends and family around the United States to find a "good therapist" for themselves or for a family member. Ideally, you would get a personal recommendation for a therapist from someone who has gone to that person, but I understand that you may (1) still have reservations about disclosing that you are looking for a therapist and (2) have wondered whether your personal business might get "leaked" to that person through the therapist. Until our community, including African Americans, Africans, and West Indians, see therapy as beneficial and not as a sign of weakness, you may choose to seek help more discreetly.

Finding an effective therapist is no easy process. Even if a therapist did good work with your best friend, she might not be a good match for you because of your different challenges or your different personalities. I do, however, have some suggestions that you might not have considered for finding the right person for you. To find an individual therapist, you may be surprised to know that your employer can help. Two ways to get referrals through your job are through employee assistance programs and health insurance providers:

- An employee assistance program (EAP) is a voluntary program offered through an employer that provides employees free and confidential assessments, short-term counseling, referrals, and follow-up services for their personal and work-related problems. Most programs provide counselors who are equipped to address issues affecting mental and emotional well-being like the ones that we have been discussing. Admittedly, I rarely hear of anyone contacting their job's EAP for referrals, but I once met an African American woman who did just that. She was very pleased with the services that she received.

- Your company's health insurance provider is another job-based resource. You may have mental health coverage, and if you do, the health insurance company will likely provide a list of mental health providers. This information is often accessible online. This is another option to get you started.

In addition to your EAP and health insurance provider, there are several Internet search options that you can conduct online to find a therapist. There are numerous online resources that detail the various types of mental health professionals. You want to look or ask specifically for "psychotherapists." If you just search "therapist," that person could actually be offering another kind of therapy, such as occupational therapy or physical therapy. The search for "counselor" typically works but is also quite broad. Your pastor is also a counselor but will not likely have training in psychotherapy. A psychotherapist provides therapy for the mind and behavior.

Therapy for Black Girls, https://www.therapyforblackgirls.com, is one online resource. Therapists provide contact information along with a photograph and brief description of their expertise. The site is not comprehensive by far, but many Black and African American therapists from across the United States have signed on to the directory.

Psychology Today magazine, https://www.psychologytoday.com/us/therapists, also provides a directory of therapists with photos and detailed credentialing. The site provides a stamp for therapists in their directory whose name, license, and contact information have been verified. Though the institution where the individual obtained the degree is listed, this information is not verified. You can verify any therapist's credentials by searching online for the state licensing board. If the person is a psychologist in Decatur, Georgia, you can search online for "psychology licensing board Georgia." For a licensed professional counselor, search "licensing board counseling Georgia." You will be able to verify the individual's license and also whether or not any complaints have been filed.

The American Psychological Association also has a psychologist locator, https://locator.apa.org. Only members of the American Psychological Association (who are presumably licensed psychologists) can be listed in the directory. Similar to the other sites, profiles include photos, and areas of expertise are detailed and identifiable using region or therapist name.

Though it is not a well-known option for mental health care, many large research universities have psychological clinics on campus that provide care to people in the community through doctoral students. Clients benefit from cutting-edge care on a sliding-fee scale. We recently had a client leave our clinic because his mother thought he should see "a psychologist." Our therapists are doctoral students who are supervised by licensed psychologists or doctoral-level professors to provide evidence-based care.

The sad reality is that not all psychologists and not all mental health providers are familiar with and trained in the best practices. In the case of the client who left the clinic, he was improving in therapy, but felt pressure to see someone who had more years of experience. Years of experience is not always a good thing. They may have graduated at a time when the latest interventions were not being taught in doctoral programs and may not have pursued training in these advanced areas since they began practicing. These are all criteria to consider when deciding on your therapist.

NAMI has been around since the 1970s as a national grassroots organization. It is a tremendous resource that provides education about mental health–related topics and advocacy for bringing attention to psychological problems. For your local NAMI, search your city or nearest metropolitan area. There are close to one thousand chapters around the United States for you to look up to see what they offer near you. Though I have not worked directly with the organization, I have known people over the years who have—people who look like you and me and who are personally invested in the community. NAMI offers free support groups that also educate family members on how to engage with someone who is suffering from mental illness.

You may benefit from group support, or you may benefit from individual therapy. If you have a family member who is diagnosed with a serious psychological problem, you may consider signing up for a free group. Even if you are the only Black person in the room, you may still benefit from sharing with others who can relate to your struggles. Suffering in isolation is much more difficult than suffering with others. Until circumstances shift, you may be the only one seeking support who looks like you. When my dad passed away, I participated in a monthly grief support group for a year. I was the only one there who had lost a parent. I was twenty-nine years old. The facilitator and all the other members of the group were white women in their sixties or older who had lost their spouse. Having someone listen to my stories about my dad was helpful. Sometimes, you just want someone to listen to you— someone who can relate somewhat to your experience and tell you that you are going to be okay.

What All Those Credentials Mean

Some therapists have doctoral degrees. Others have master's degrees. All must be licensed to practice in their state, meaning that, in addition to having the degree, they have passed national and state exams and participate in continuing education. The variety of credentials illustrate that there are different areas of expertise and approaches to training. Nevertheless, all therapists are expected to obtain a license in the state in which they are practicing. That license should be visible to you in the therapist's office.

Your needs and preferences will determine who is the most qualified professional for you. Most available practitioners have master's level degrees. They may be licensed professional counselors (LPC) and licensed mental health counselors (LMHC) or obtain licensure as an MFT, a marriage and family therapist. These individuals have completed master's degree level coursework in psychology, counseling, or marriage and family therapy and obtained the required number of supervised clinical hours before being authorized to see clients independently. Licensed clinical social workers (LCSW) are also credentialed at the master's degree level and provide individual, family, and group therapy. Psychiatric nurse practitioners provide mental health services and are often affiliated with a medical center or hospital. There are providers who specialize in treatment of substance-use problems who may not have graduate degrees but have earned a certification to practice.

Licensed psychologists have typically earned doctoral-level PhDs or PsyDs. PhD programs in psychology are highly competitive and require that students balance learning skills to work with psychotherapy clients and understanding and developing research (whereby they are immersed in the science of mental health). PsyD programs primarily emphasize expertise in psychological testing and psychotherapy, though some also engage in research.

A good therapist can be challenging to find in part because two people can come from the same training program and still differ in their ability to be helpful. While individuals who obtain doctoral degrees have trained longer, there are talented individuals at the master's degree level who could provide a perfect fit for your emotional health needs. I know psychiatric nurses who have fewer years of formal training than people with doctoral degrees, but those nurses can lead even the most troubled person to a better life. One of my out-of-state friends recently sent me a list of three psychotherapists that interested her. I selected one that appeared to be the youngest of the three; my selection was due to my familiarity with her competitive training program and its evidence base for training clinicians. My friend complained that she looked young, but I reminded her that (1) Black don't crack and (2) the psychologist's seeming youth could also mean that she is trained in the most up-to-date therapeutic approaches.

Finally, don't confuse psychiatrists and psychologists. The distinction is important to your search for therapy versus medication and other medical interventions. Psychiatrists are doctors of medicine (MDs) who prescribe medication, while psychologists typically earn

PhDs. Psychiatrists are specifically trained in the use of medicine to improve mental health. The medications that influence brain functioning are known as "psychotropics." Some psychiatrists also provide talk therapy, but the majority do not. In most states, psychologists cannot prescribe medications.

In some ways, finding a therapist can be a dice roll, but review their personal websites for their expertise and what they offer to clients. It may also take some of the pressure off of your search if you know that the provider that you begin with may not be the provider that you end up with. Once you decide that you want professional help, the last thing that you may feel you have time or energy for is shopping around. However, I point out that you are not bound to stay with a therapist in the same way that you are not bound to stay with a physician who is not meeting your needs. Make a list of three possible therapist options from the start.

What to Expect in Therapy

If you have never been in therapy before, you may not know what to expect. Know also that each therapist is different. There are lots of depictions of fictional psychotherapists on television and in the movies. My favorite movie therapist of all time is Sean Maguire played by Robin Williams in *Good Will Hunting*. Will Hunting was court-ordered to therapy to avoid jail time. He had already run off "award-winning" therapists when he was introduced to Sean Maguire. For the first couple of sessions, Sean sat in silence with his client, in an effort to meet his client where he was. I attempt to instill this in therapists in training. If you show up to session in emotional pain and your therapist rushes to get you to feel better without understanding your pain, your values, or your reservation about being in therapy, you are much less likely to develop a good rapport.

Rapport is the positive, trusting, working relationship between the therapist and the client that is at the foundation of therapy success. All of psychological science tells us that it is the most important (but not the only) factor in whether you are able to meet your therapy goals. The available science suggests that rapport is more important than therapist expertise. Though Sean Maguire was an experienced therapist in *Good Will Hunting*, what set him apart was his creative and flexible capacity to meet a very challenging client where he was. Though Sean's approach to therapy was fairly unstructured, it was helpful for the character in the movie. At the same time, if you rely on television and movies as your source of insight to how therapy goes, you may be misled. Though less structured approaches to therapy do occur and are popular in certain parts of the United States (and on television), structured approaches are more effective.

In the very first session of structured therapy, your new therapist begins by discussing confidentiality and limits to confidentiality, expectations about cancellations, and other logistics. In the first session, the therapist will obtain background information from you (e.g., work, level of education, living situation, etc.). She will ask what it is that brings you in for therapy. Also in the first session, the therapist talks to you about her approach to therapy. The amount of information that the therapist shares about herself will vary but will be relatively limited in the interest of focusing more on you. If you prefer to ask questions of the therapist to feel more comfortable, you can do so. These are some of the questions you may have.

What is your approach to psychotherapy? In the first session, the therapist needs to describe her understanding of how problems come about and how best to solve them through therapy. Therapists are trained in various approaches, and we understand the source of the problem based on our training. As an example, some might assume that current problems are based on unresolved issues from your upbringing versus others who focus on how you see the world today. As a result, we propose different solutions based on how we understand the problem. My own approach to therapy is cognitively oriented, and the therapy or interventions that I supervise fall in the realm of "cognitive behavioral" work that addresses problems that arise due to how people think about the world around them. Some therapists see clients' challenges as evolving from childhood relationships that require some working through. If a client came to our clinic with such a goal, we would be limited in our capacity to provide them services. Childhood concerns often impact current thinking, but we would focus on the current thinking more so than the poor relationship with a parent.

How does the therapist know where to begin? Your new therapist will often ask you questions until she understands what is troubling you and your expectations for what life will look like when you have completed therapy. Your expectations are tied to your *goals*. Most clients go to therapy wanting life to be different or better but do not often have a specific goal in mind. Your therapist can help you zero in on a goal if she has a sense of the problem, but ideally, this is a collaborative effort. Just because you say that you are tired and frustrated does not mean that your fatigue is the same as the last client's fatigue. It may take a couple of sessions to break down what all is really going on.

How long will this take? This will vary…a lot. It is unlikely that any actual "change" would take place in the first session. However, the therapist may ask you questions that will cause you to seriously evaluate your life situation and give you a different perspective and new insight. Consider that you go to therapy because you have been feeling desperately unhappy with your life for years. Your therapist asks when it was that you first began to feel so unhappy. You respond that work is on track and your children are healthy and thriving. However, the despair has been building for ten years or more. You might add that your despair is worse when you have major disagreements with your spouse. Until you answered the therapist's question, you did not realize that you have felt trapped and depressed for fourteen years in your marriage (like a frog in a cool pot). You knew that you were not satisfied but did not previously consider how this dissatisfaction could be affecting you.

Over the course of therapy, you and your therapist will work together to address the unhappiness that brought you to therapy. You'll do so in a way that makes sense to you. At agreed-upon intervals, you can evaluate how things are going. To be most effective, you will want to be as open as you can possibly be so the therapist understands the true nature of your problems. You will also want to complete any assignments, tasks, or homework that the therapist advises.

All Therapy Is Not the Same

All therapists are not equal. Also, all therapies are not equal and will not achieve the same results. Therapy has evolved in the same way that other aspects of society have evolved. At one time in your life, you may have connected to the internet using a slow modem that beeped and honked until you were "online." Now, thanks to wireless technology, the internet is literally in the air. With continuous technological advances, who knows what will show up next. This is the case with therapy.

Researchers have determined that given certain types of problems, certain therapies are much more effective than others. In evidence-based practice (EBP), psychological scientists have tested different approaches to specific types of problems. I add a caveat here that some of these researchers have rarely if ever published research on the usefulness of an intervention with African Americans. Most researchers assume that the research findings apply regardless of race. In many cases, they will, but therapy that has evidence to support it does not mean that the evidence is strong. However, if you consider a therapist who has expertise in treating a certain type of problem that has been debilitating for you, you can ask if she uses EBP and if not, what is her approach. I can say with confidence that if you have been managing depression most days of the week for many months, an evidence-based intervention is the best option for you. If you have not been able to heal yourself from social anxiety, evidence-based practice that involves "exposure" is the best approach.

Not everyone is using evidence-based intervention. In the clinic where I supervise client cases, it is not unusual for a client to say that they received services elsewhere, but that the services were not helpful. They might also say that the therapy was helpful, but they cannot describe a single thing that they actively did other than talk. These are clients who have issues that are diagnosable psychological problems and meet what we call a threshold for impacting daily life. They would benefit from structured, evidence-based therapy. If you have depression and feelings of hopelessness that keep you from enjoying being out with your friends and concentrating at work and you are wondering if life is worth living, a therapist might suggest a cognitive therapy approach or she might suggest "behavioral activation" in which you get moving with specific activities.

For depression, evidence-based therapies seem to have longer-lasting effects than medication alone. For some, however, the depression is so seriously ingrained in the individual that it is challenging to implement and benefit from such intervention without medication.

Cognitive behavioral therapy, or CBT, is my preferred approach to addressing life challenges. If you're experiencing excessive worry, problems sleeping, overeating, and even unexplained pain in your body, there is a CBT intervention. Because depression and anxiety are the most commonly occurring psychological problems, they have the most developed interventions. As an example, interpersonal therapy focuses on the individual's relationships with others as well as the initial trigger for the depression (which has implications for current relationships). A therapist might use relaxation techniques to help with stress management and difficulties sleeping or problem-focused therapy as a strategy to manage depressive responses to life circumstances that may seem to be out of your control. Part of being a competent therapist is that she must work with you to match the therapy to your life circumstances. For some people, cognitive work is less effective than assigning you to go for a walk. It may sound simple, but the science shows that for some people, going for a walk is good medicine.

Depending on their training, most therapists can assist you in developing tools to manage life stress. However, some therapists have expertise in specific areas. Alcohol and drug abuse, trauma, and certain types of anxiety, such as obsessive-compulsive disorder, which we discussed in chapter 4, are areas in which therapists can specialize. If you see someone for a specific psychological disorder for which they are not trained to use evidence-based practice, you may walk away dissatisfied. Because of the delicate nature of trauma and traumatic responses, I would advise that you find someone who specializes or has expertise in that area. Advising you to "not think about it" is not therapy. The same is true if you or a loved one struggles with alcohol abuse. These are challenging problems to treat. Someone who specializes in the area will know what to look for and how best to navigate you through the difficult work ahead.

I should mention that while there is help for a lot of different emotional health challenges, you want to be aware that some types of problems are less "treatable." You may have encountered people who would qualify as having a *personality disorder*. These are diagnosable problems, but the individuals have a way of relating to other people that can be especially problematic because they have very little, if any, insight into how frustrating, infuriating, or annoying they are to other people. Perhaps your ex-fiancé who was so immersed in his own importance to the exclusion of you or anyone else met criteria for narcissistic personality disorder. Your childhood friend who (bless her heart) is in one unstable relationship after another, always seems to make impulsive decisions, and has extreme emotional reactions could be diagnosed with borderline personality disorder. The reality is that whether that person benefits from psychotherapy or not, you can choose how much of your PF can be sacrificed for your relationship with them.

You May Have to See a White Therapist

In a perfect world and if you prefer one, you will find a Black therapist, well trained in providing mental health services and dedicated to elevating your psychological fortitude. Because therapy relationships are so important, you may feel that you can only trust and be comfortable with a Black therapist. This feeling is absolutely understandable. You would not want to subject yourself to yet another "space" where you have to pretend to not be you, avoid your African American vernacular to speak standard English or even worse, have your therapist act like she doesn't see you as Black. Finding a Black therapist might be ideal. But ethnicity is not the only criteria, or the most important, for you to consider. Your Black therapist might be nice, but if she has no experience with trauma, your capacity to improve will be limited. The therapy might feel good because she is a great listener in a way that no one else in your life listens, but you won't address the trouble that your trauma has been causing you.

There are white therapists who are perfectly fine seeing a Black client. This is important because when you are struggling emotionally, the last thing that you want to do is see a therapist who is uncomfortable around Black people. However, I assure you that there are therapists out there who would be good at establishing a relationship with you. You are best served if you do your homework, get reliable referrals, and research your options.

As you might expect, most therapists are white women. The mental health system is, in many of ways, a microcosm of our larger society. Not everyone is "culturally competent" and able to demonstrate their ability to work with individuals who are culturally different from them. To my knowledge, graduate programs in clinical psychology do not admit doctoral students based on their capacity to not be racist. The assumption is that they are admitted with some common sense not to be racist in our field of psychology and that they will learn to demonstrate cultural competence while in graduate training. Most accredited programs, at least in psychology, embrace cultural competence as an objective. That means that students in training take a course or two in multicultural psychology and are expected to be able to successfully navigate the nuances of working with clients who are Black, Asian, Latinx/Hispanic, LGBTQ2, or from a lower income bracket—any reality that impacts how the client experiences the world that is not a mainstream, middle-class, Eurocentric lens. For some, a course or two with practice seeing clients from diverse backgrounds is sufficient.

If you find that a white therapist may be your only option, you can assess whether or not that person could be a good fit for you. Ask what percentage of her clients have been African American or Jamaican or who are first-generation United States citizens. If the question elicits discomfort, that might be all the data that you need to move on to the next therapist on your list.

Mainstream psychology treats cultural competence as a place where we *arrive* as professionals. We either check the competence box or we do not. It is better, however, for a therapist to recognize that he or she is continually evolving and must be open to that process. Given the success that you have had in navigating predominantly white work settings, you have a sense of whether or not a white person has some "humility" about their whiteness. It does not mean that they will not make any missteps. However, they certainly won't make any egregious mistakes, like trying to touch your hair in the first session or insisting that the microaggression that you experienced was in your head. You want to know that your therapist will be genuinely receptive when you give her feedback about her interactions with you. Therapists who aspire to cultural humility are willing to be critical of themselves. They are flexible and willing to learn more about you and, importantly, what your culture means to you. They also obtain information without relying solely on you as a sole source of knowledge.

What If You Need Medication?

Prescription medication can help you get out of a rut so you can benefit from therapy. A chemical imbalance is difficult to overcome on your own. If you have been in therapy for months or years with tremendous difficulty achieving small goals despite having a well-trained therapist, there is a chance that you could benefit from medication.

You may not need medication, but if you do, it is best prescribed and managed by a psychiatrist. They can work with you to figure out if an antidepressant, anti-anxiety, or other psychotropic prescription could be helpful for you. Your primary care physician can also prescribe medication. In fact, primary care doctors prescribe a significant proportion of anti-anxiety and antidepressant medication in part because people are more likely to see their doctor and not follow up with a psychiatrist. However, determining prescription medication can be a delicate process. There are various medications that could have different side effects. The doctor will do their best to find the right medication type for you.

If you tell your doctor that you have been so stressed that you have difficulties sleeping at night and find yourself being overly worried about your work performance during the day, she may prescribe something that ends up making you feel strange and jittery as a side effect. If you are tempted to stop taking your prescription after one week, let the professional who prescribed the medication know about the uncomfortable side effects. Call the office, and speak to the nurse. Do not keep your experience to yourself and simply discontinue your medication. Take time to figure out what works for you.

There are a number of different types of medication. A psychiatrist would be best equipped to consider alternative psychotropic medications and at the appropriate dosage. Also, if you are on other medications, the psychiatrist can problem solve if your medications are impacting one another. Perhaps the lorazepam that your psychiatrist prescribed would be better for you at a lower dosage. On the other hand, it may work right away at the initial prescription. You may begin to notice new energy and a renewed sense of focus that you never knew could exist for you. You might wonder why you did not consider antidepressant medication sooner.

If you are just beginning to think about improving your psychological fortitude and strongly dislike medications, it is okay to begin with "talk therapy," whereby you work through your problems with a psychologist or licensed professional counselor. Sometimes, psychologists will recommend the addition of medication to your regimen after a period of time. Often, I find that people who say that they oppose medication and therapy will take Tylenol PM several nights per week to fall asleep. For some reason, they don't have any concerns with over-the-counter meds. If this sounds like you, it could be a sign that you want a quick fix instead of real change. Please commit to challenging your biases so you can make the best decision for your health and well-being. When it comes to your very complex psychological fortitude, the perfect formula may take some time to figure out. You might as well put some effort toward finding a solution.

Change Cannot Be Amazon-Primed

Therapy is not magical. It does not work overnight. If you go into a session thinking that you will be healed of your ills inside of two weeks, you will be disappointed. When you decide to see a professional, you may be at the height of distress or at your lowest psychological fortitude. The therapist's first responsibility is to establish a relationship with you and gain some insight about what is going on for you, how the problem came to be, and what you have done to manage it.

Sometimes the problem came to be over decades. The therapist may have to uncover decades of hurt in order to understand your current problem. What this looks like is that you address one problem, but then another seems to emerge unexpectedly. What is important about this is that you would not expect someone to fix your car without diagnosing what the car is doing that it's not supposed to do, how the problem came about, and whether or not you did anything to address the problem.

However, if there is a chance that you would not return to that therapist because you do not think she can help you, it is best that you let the therapist know up front. In doing so, the therapist can take time to determine what might be done to fix your most pressing problem (because there is often more than one) or let you know what additional information is needed to address that problem. In any case, follow your instincts. If you do not feel comfortable with the therapist, you can let her know that it is not working out. If you are comfortable, but feeling antsy, you may want to settle in for a while. For therapy in general, plan on no less than twelve to sixteen sessions, but this depends on your level of distress and your willingness to work on assigned tasks outside of session.

Step Outside Your Box for Higher PF

You can get professional help—whether you are addressing a serious disorder or you are hoping to increase your psychological fortitude. If you feel isolated and just need to be heard because no one is listening to you, it may be helpful to talk to someone who can provide you with support. You may even consider a group. For some people, supportive therapy is helpful.

Perhaps you have experienced countless years of being dissatisfied with life. You thought that once you achieved the promotion or once you retired or once your children graduated from high school, things would be different. By now, everyone has graduated college and retirement has come and gone, but you are as dissatisfied with life as you have ever been. You will likely have to go out of your comfort zone to find the help that you need, but therapy will help you with a new and different perspective and give you some tools for coping. Help may not come in the form that you are seeking, but if you are flexible, a psychology professional can be beneficial at any stage of life.

CHAPTER 11

Apply New and Improved Tools to Overcome Stress

You had expectations for your life and what it was going to look like. In high school, you had plans to go to college, get your business degree, get married, and have your perfect son and daughter by the time you were thirty years old (and definitely by now). You did not expect that it would be so hard to save money to start your business. Of course, you had to start working right out of college so you could pay back those student loans. Now you are almost thirty or forty or fifty or sixty years old and feeling like "what's the point?" It seems you have wasted time. You thought about going back to school to get your MBA but talked yourself out of creating new student loans and getting back into debt. You can't maintain your quality of life if you go back to school. If only you had gotten better mentoring. If only your parents had helped you with your tuition. If only you had gotten that big bonus last year. If only you knew about your PF sooner. Life just hasn't been fair.

Everyone around you seems to be doing *way better* than you are. They are so happy with their lives that they could not imagine that you could be so miserable. No one would believe that there are days when you have fleeting thoughts of some type of accident just to get some relief from your misery. You go to church and read Bible scriptures but feeling better is always temporary. The dating scene is pitiful. The men that you meet have no capacity for conversation. You could stand to lose a few pounds, but you still cute. The universe must be plotting against you. You wonder why you just can't be happy like everybody else.

Some Things Truly Are Out of Your Control

You can continue your route to more fortitude by not beating yourself up about things in your past that were out of your control. If getting a job was the only way for you to pay off those loans, you made the best decision that you knew to make. If your parents or your grandmother did not give you the money, that is not your fault. The fact that Mr. Right has not shown up is just that. We were all sold a fairy tale about what life is supposed to be like. You're smart enough to create a new one for yourself. You cannot do this if your head is out of the game and you are sabotaging your psychological fortitude by looking backward.

If you are honest with yourself, you will see that although all these obstacles are real, it is you who has decided that they are insurmountable. With a little shift in perspective and internal reassessment, you can begin to see things differently and move yourself toward your best life. Even if you decide that you need help, it's going to be up to you to take the steps to get help and engage other tools like the ones in this chapter.

If your psychological fortitude is low because you are overextended on your responsibilities—running your children around town and trying to keep up with the Johnsons—the tools I share will have limited effect for you. Your remedy is found in chapter 9 because you need to call in family and friends as reinforcements and learn to do less.

I also caution that you run the risk of feeling better and then completely undoing your progress. The tricky nature of psychological fortitude and all aspects of mental and emotional health is that as soon as we begin to feel even a little bit better, we tend to return to some of the behaviors that diminished our psychological fortitude in the first place. You raise your psychological fortitude from 60 to 70 only to overextend yourself even further; you are feeling better, so you take on too much again. I recommend that you seek to gain some relief right now in ways I will introduce in this chapter (together with strategies that I suggested in chapter 8 on spirituality). You can also seek someone to talk to, whether a trusted friend or clergy member or a professional therapist or group, who can help you maintain long-term progress.

When You Must Take Time Off for Yourself, Call in Black

"Evelyn from the Internets" introduced me to this phenomenal idea in one of her most popular YouTube videos "Call in Black." (If you don't already enjoy her videos, search for her YouTube channel or try this link: https://www.youtube.com/watch?v=cpVeUVcFMAU.) In the video, she addresses the trauma of dealing with the murders of unarmed Black people by police. She says the toll that it takes on Black people can be too much to go to work. I agree.

When you are not feeling physically well, you call in sick so you can feel better and return to work with the capacity to get your job done. In the same way, when you are overwhelmed by the reality of navigating racism in our society, you can call in Black so you can stay home to stop your head from spinning or at least not worsen it with the fatigue of racism—racism to which few others (if any) in your office can relate.

Despite how far we have come, when we work in a space where we are the only one or one of a very few African Americans, when we feel compelled to use standard English with just the right amount of sing-song in our voice to be as nonthreatening as possible, we are still on the plantation. The workplace is often controlled by white men and in a manner that is dismissive or sometimes demeaning. On the plantation, we never expect to be listened to or have our ideas affirmed. Even if the person in charge looks like you, he identifies with the slave master and not with you. It may be uncomfortable to call that out, but so much of our efforts are spent operating in an alternate universe, we might as well acknowledge reality for the sake of our psychological fortitude. In the world of psychology, pretending that anything exists, that actually does not—and vice versa—is evidence of losing touch with reality. Psychologically, losing touch with reality is a problem.

For your fortitude, you need to have a sister or brother in your struggles. Such a connection keeps you grounded. Do you remember the scene from the *Color Purple* when Celie sees her sister, Nettie, for the first time since they were teenagers? Many memes have been made of this embrace. My favorite is the one for "when you work with five hundred white people and you finally see the new Black person that they hired in the hallway." It means so much to have another person to connect with in spaces where there is inherent oppression. If your African Americanness has any meaning to you at all, this is true for even the most progressive of workplaces where you are less than 5 percent of employees. Assuming that you are not competing with her as the only other Black employee, she can be a source of respite. She is someone who "gets" life on the plantation.

If you do not have a Nettie, you might have to use your paid vacations days from time to time to call in Black. Call them "sick" days if you like, but your physical symptoms, such as headache or fatigue, are often stress-related. Give yourself a break from wearing a mask, through which you present yourself as acceptable on the plantation. It is inauthentic, and it is tiring.

You do not need an excuse to take care of your well-being. If you have a career, you probably have at least two jobs…or more. Once you leave the office plantation, you have to go home to your second full-time job—taking care of your responsibilities to your family. And if you are an officer in one of your civic organizations or your alumni association, you have two and a half jobs. Then add yet another job to this pressure cooker if you are the only Black person or the only Black woman in your office. Because it's a lot of work to manage the "impostor syndrome" and the subtle messages that you receive—from others and yourself—that you are not good enough to be there. Now, add a final job for your psyche to handle: the weight that descends when yet another Black child has been murdered by police for holding a bag of candy.

The totality of your many jobs can weigh on you more than you can bear. Let's make a deal: If you are holding on to all your paid time off for a rainy day, don't. If you are someone who loses your sick time, stop. Call in Black. Being Black is hard work. Do not hang out in that pot of cool water while the temperature slowly increases and you find that you are cooked like that frog before you know it.

Do you need an excuse? Your psychological fortitude dipped below 75 because you spent hours working on your son's school project the night before it was due. Perhaps you were on the phone all night with your sister trying to problem solve her custody situation with her ex-husband. Just last week, your brother was in jail and needed you to go get him out. Maybe you were handling all of this just fine, but then you found out that a grand jury did not indict an officer who shot an unarmed mother in front of her child not too far from where you work. There. That's your personal excuse, even if it's not the one you give to your boss on the phone when you call in to take the day off. Stay home and listen to "Feeling Good" or anything else by Nina Simone.

After a while, life challenges add up. Everyone has a tipping point. It says nothing bad about you if you take some time for yourself. Taking time for yourself is *your most important responsibility*. Don't let the habit of putting yourself last get so entrenched that you forget why you do it.

In-the-Moment Tools to Boost Psychological Fortitude

You may have figured out that you have some symptoms of anxiety or depression. You may, or may not, decide that you do not have enough to "see someone" like a professional counselor or a therapist, but you can honestly admit that you have some signs or symptoms.

You have accomplished so much on your own that you can surely figure out how to take care of your own mind. You can raise your own psychological fortitude a few points when you are good and ready to do so. Let's get you going to decrease some of your worry or sad mood in the moment.

If your goal is to feel better and stronger right now *and* to build your psychological fortitude going forward, I suggest that you think of your efforts in these two ways:

- How can I increase my PF in *this* moment?

- How can I build toward sustaining higher psychological fortitude by applying these tools more often?

As you apply the suggestions and tools I offer, take time to make some improvements, and begin to see some positive results, sit with those gains for a period (three months, perhaps) before you even consider overwhelming yourself again by adding tasks.

Tool 1: You Already Breathe, Just Breathe Deeper

One of my favorite things to do is introduce people to breathing exercises. With some of what you have been dealing with, you might be thinking, *What does deep breathing do?* or *I already breathe.* I can imagine your suspicion about something as simple as breathing. If you already meditate or do yoga, you are ahead of the game. This is a refresher. If not, it will be a handy new tool for you.

Breathing deeply is one of the simplest, but most important, things that you can do to increase psychological fortitude. It is simple because you can do it anywhere. There are only two things that can limit its effectiveness:

- Trying to do it "perfectly." Because you have to retrain your breathing, the overachiever in you will be so focused on getting it "just right" that you will overthink it and perhaps berate yourself for not getting it right. If you struggle for perfect breathing, you will have already missed the point of the activity.

- Remembering to do it at crucial moments. A crucial moment is when you are overwhelmed, do not know what to do, and need to put yourself in mental time-out before you make a decision or do something that will not help you in the long run.

Breathing deeply takes you out of the moment when you are most stressed about what is happening around you. Oftentimes, we just need to be removed from a situation in order to gain a fresh, and perhaps different, perspective on what's going on.

Deep breathing is also good for your health because it limits your body's stress response, which is regulated by your sympathetic and parasympathetic nervous systems. When you are overwhelmed by stress, your heart rate increases and your blood pressure rises as part of your sympathetic nervous system. Some have likened it to the gas pedal in your automobile. Press the pedal and all systems go! It is a natural response to stress that can become unnatural if you experience ongoing stress that you do not manage. Breathing deeply allows the parasympathetic nervous system to be activated like a brake pedal, which calms you down and refreshes your view. You are forced to do something that most adults are bad at doing for the body—slow down to take oxygen into the body appropriately.

Think about when your doctor tells you to take a deep breath. You do so like a good student (or so you think). Your chest expands and lifts as far as you can get it to go. However, deep breathing is not about expanding your chest. It is about breathing from your belly. Deep breathing is about getting oxygen in your body directed where it is supposed to go. If you ever notice a baby in a crib, her little belly looks like it has a balloon in it that is inflating and deflating over and over again. This is how we as adults are supposed to breathe, but we have gotten lazy with our breathing over time. When you have a moment to put the book or your app down, put one hand on your chest and one hand on your tummy, and take a deep breath. Which moved more? Your chest or your tummy? You want your tummy to move more.

Why? Because there is going to come a time when you travel to your hometown for a wedding, holiday, or funeral. All of the usual suspects are there. You love your family, but being around all of them at the same time is just too much. Deep breathing helps manage your reactions and protect your PF. Maybe you need to use your deep breathing more often than just big family occasions. You have to go to that job of yours where you are the only Black woman as far as the eye can see. You wish you could blink yourself out of a room no less than two times each week. It is not unusual for you to have a headache by the end of the day, but the ibuprofen (and the separate bottle in your workbag) takes away the pain but not the stress. When any difficult moments arise, even when you encounter your nemesis in the elevator, take a deep breath.

Feel free to search YouTube for "deep breathing exercises." There are different approaches, so find one that walks you through methods that work best for you. Your goal is to be able to focus on your own body and your own breathing. Watch the video, but then close your eyes and practice for yourself. Practice is what will help you remember to take a deep breath in the midst of life's stressors.

Tool 2: Cut Off the Useless Things You Say to Yourself

Another important tool is for you to check your self-talk. Here's how self-talk works. Imagine you and your mom are walking through a mall. You see one of her old friends. You both wave "hello," but the woman does not wave back to you. You assume that the woman did not see you. You shrug it off. But your mom insists that this "friend" did see the two of you and chose to ignore you both. Your mom is salty about it. She goes on and on for a while about her triflin' friend. Though you and your mom saw the situation very differently, the woman's behavior did not change. You and your mom saw the same thing, but there was a big difference in how you each interpreted it—and you each *felt differently* as a result. These two interpretations of the same "nonwave" led to different feelings.

This self-talk business is crucial to your psychological fortitude. We all *interpret* what situations mean, for better or worse, often not seeing them for what they are. We often just don't have access to the whole story—in fact, we rarely do! Remember the waitress who treated you poorly the other day? You paid good money for your food but couldn't know she was distracted by a sick child or mother at home.

We can all work to improve how we see ourselves and the people around us in ways that support our fortitude. Psychologists and other mental health professionals call this work "cognitive restructuring." The goal is to change your stressful thinking and replace it with a less stressful way of seeing everyday situations. Your mother might argue, "But I know she saw us," and you might insist, "I know that waitress was acting funky because she didn't want to serve us." Both could be true. The question is, is it worth your psychological fortitude to be right, or could you assume that you might be missing part of the picture? In the interest of not letting the situation rob you of enjoying a lovely meal or rob your mom of special time with her grown daughter, choose the self-talk that supports your peace of mind.

There are a number of ways that we interpret situations and then talk to ourselves as if our interpretations are fact. In the end, it's less than helpful but happens all the time. I will share a few that I observe too often in Black women like you—women who are winning in corporate America, moving hearts and souls in entertainment, and managing households where everyone seems to be in their right minds. But somehow, useless thoughts such as these persist.

Disqualifying the positive. Despite everything that you have going for you, you feel dissatisfied with life. Here are some of the many ways you may live this out in your head.

- You have a good job that pays well and makes you the pride of your family. But you are woefully disappointed that you aren't more advanced in your career.

- You're divorced and have been dating a really good guy for about a year. He treats you and your son well. But you agonize over why he has not proposed to you.

- You have a home that others seem to envy. In fact, friends are always asking you to help them decorate. You question why anyone would ask for your help.

- You have great friends in your life, but they are overscheduled. Since you do not get to go out with them as much as you would like, you often feel lonely and friendless.

- You would like to lose fifteen pounds to get back to your college weight, but your doctor says that you are in good health. Rather than accepting your good health, you focus on those "dimples" in your thighs.

Rather than seeing all of the wonderful things in your life and on a daily basis, you find ways to see the negative more often than the positive. At best, your psychological fortitude is 65.

Mind reading. You typically make negative assumptions about what people are thinking and what they mean when they say something. An honest conversation would save you some grief in any one of these scenarios:

- Your only regular activity is going to church on Sundays and even then, you keep to yourself. You would like to meet new people and be active, but you are certain that no one wants to be friends with a sixty-year-old woman. They will probably just wonder what is wrong with you that you do not have anyone to spend time with. It is also possible that they will be happy to meet a new friend and hear new ideas for things to do.

- Since retirement, you find that you just don't know what to do with yourself. More than anything, you eat when you are not hungry to keep your mind busy. Your son and daughter have suggested everything from moving into a retirement community to finding opportunities to volunteer. But instead of seeing how they are worried that you are by yourself so much, you assume they don't think you can take care of yourself anymore.

- You thought about going to a book club meeting for African American women but changed your mind because you never went to college. And when you tried to meet with women from church, most of them had college degrees and seemed to look down on you. They had to be thinking how simple you are. Can you recall what it was that they said to suggest they looked down on you? Unless they explicitly said this, the reality is that you have no idea what they think about you.

- You worked your way up from an unpaid internship to management, but you're certain you never made the executive team because you just know the CEO didn't like you. When he said that the company would support you to get an MBA, is it possible that he wanted to invest in you so you could join the executive team and not that he thought something was wrong with you?

You are a mind reader. It is not a good superpower to have. While you may be good at "reading" people, understanding their hidden intentions, and making calculated moves as a result, the kind of mind reading that I am describing is (really) bad for your PF. Are there naysayers at the church? Yes. Are there people out there who think they are better than you? Yes. Do any of these mean anything about who you are and what you need for your life? No.

A therapist who is trained in cognitive behavioral therapy will have strategies to help you meet your goal of reducing negative self-talk. David Burns is also a great resource if you want to read more about "disqualifying the positive" and other less than helpful ways of thinking in his classic book *Feeling Good: The New Mood Therapy*.[40] In the meantime, here are some steps that you can take.

Step 1: Notice it. One clue to a deeply ingrained self-talk is that someone says something that you "feel a certain way about" or you feel a certain way before they even say it.

Step 2: Acknowledge it for what it is: negativity. You could be right about your thought, but does being right help your PF in this context?

Step 3: Have a little chat with the negativity inside your head. You have permission to evaluate what is most important. Do you prefer to assume that your thought is correct and sabotage your own well-being? Or do you want to explore other options? Begin by thinking of what else might be true, or let go by realizing there are things you don't know about the situation.

Step 4: Make a decision. Decide that you want optimal fortitude for yourself. Replace your negative talk with more positive ways of thinking about your world and the people around you. This is a skill that is built up gradually moment by moment, thought by thought. So keep at it.

Tool 3: Stop "Shoulding" on Yourself

If I could, I would absolutely remove the word "should" from every dictionary. Its only purpose is to make you feel bad. Think about it. You say "should" to motivate yourself, like, "I should eat healthier," or "I should work on my business plan." It may very well be true that eating better and working on your business plan are your goals, but if you have not been doing either, I am sure that there is a good reason. Maybe you do not eat better because you need to plan your meals and go to the grocery store to prepare those meals. If you have not made time for either of these tasks, how are you going to eat better? Saying that you "should" only makes you feel worse because you are doing the best that you can with, let's say, your limited time and options. Until you free up the time and carry out a plan, there is no benefit to shoulding on yourself.

You rack up double distress points when you should on other people. You say things like, "They *should* call and check on me sometime." "My husband *should* help me out more around the house." "Given all that I do for my family, they *should* appreciate me more." These are just a handful of examples of how shoulds do nothing but make you resentful that people you care about don't seem to care about you.

I encourage you to pay attention to how you use the word "should." As far as I am concerned, there is no reason for you to ever use it. It will take time, but you can remove it from your vocabulary because it will just make you feel bad. Usually, you can replace "should" with "it would be helpful."

- "It would be helpful if my spouse cleaned the kitchen more."

- "It would be helpful if I can get my business plan together."

- "It would help me feel less frustrated with all that I have to do if my family appreciated what I do accomplish."

This simple language change removes the guilt from what you or someone else is not doing. I find it hilarious that, when I talk to an audience about removing the word "should" from their vocabulary, someone ends up using it in a question or comment right away. Some have an immediate awareness while others wonder why members of the audience are chuckling. We have no idea how ingrained our use of "should" is, along with its negative expectations. So please, do not try to remove the word right away. Just be aware of it, if possible. The first step is to recognize the problem. You can work by yourself or with the help of a therapist to improve how you see yourself and the people around you.

When "Simple" Is Not So Simple

Honestly, if these strategies were so simple, you would have come up with them on your own. Even better, you would be able to use them as soon as you put this book down. But, in truth, they are not that simple. The tools are "simple" in the sense that anyone can use them. Anyone. They don't require complicated steps or significant time commitments. But they are not simple because they require a change in the way you are currently doing things and thinking about yourself. And change (sometimes even small change) is never easy and often doesn't feel simple. You might have an expectation that the tools will magically work on their own—as if you were not the one in control of them. Unfortunately, you *are* in control. If you are having difficulty with using the deep breathing, recognizing your negative self-talk, or rephrasing your "shouldisms," the problem could be either your autopilot or limited motivation—or both.

Overcome Your Autopilot to Regain Control Over Your Decisions

Think about this: if you work outside of the home in the same office building, Monday through Friday, you know what autopilot is. It is grabbing your keys, getting in the car to drive home from work knowing that your husband texted you to stop by the grocery store before you get home. You intend to make the turn into the store parking lot, but you miss your turn. How did that happen? He texted you right before you got in the car. It wasn't intentional that you didn't stop at the store.

You were on autopilot. You always drive the same route. You know how to miss that annoying pothole. You even know that if you get caught at the light at a certain intersection, you'll be sitting a long time for the light to change. This is part of your routine. You don't think about it. Your brain is like that. It is wired to adapt with repetition.

You just read that you need to remove the word "should" from your vocabulary. I even gave you a substitute to use. In fact, I said you don't have to remove it right away. Just notice it. Why? I know how hard it is to remember to make the turn to the grocery store. It made sense when you were reading about "shoulding" on yourself, but shoulding is just what you do.

Say you are a stay-at-home mom who is responsible for most or all of the housecleaning and cooking for the family most days. You also know what autopilot is. If you had to think about every single little thing that you do, you would go mad. You have good intentions, but once your daughter arrives home from school, that signals the beginning of overdrive. You're in autopilot to get the homework completed, the meal finished, and heaven forbid there is a social studies project due. You go into autopilot just to survive with your mind halfway intact. Who wouldn't?

To get some real change, you are going to have to integrate some tools into your autopilot. Noticing and then avoiding negative self-talk or "should" requires some deliberate action on your part. Here are some ideas:

- Put a sticky note on your bathroom mirror, laptop, or the refrigerator door to remind yourself to notice. If you prefer discretion, write the letter S and tell your family that it stands for "superwoman," who sees the positive and shoulds no more.

- See how often your children say "should," which may reflect your own use. But before you correct their usage, stop yourself when you feel an urge to should on yourself or others.

- Create a reminder on your cell phone. If you "should" a lot, you likely keep a list of things you should do. Take time to add a reminder to notice your should approximately three times per day—after your daughter is off to school, at lunch hour, and just before everyone is expected home at the end of the day.

You are really, really going to have to practice your self-awareness if you are determined not to get help from a therapist. When you are ready, you can take small steps. Every bit of effort matters. Instead of giving yourself a hard time for not being ready, just admit that you are not there yet and remain open for the moment when you are.

Motivation—Knowing Better and Doing Better

My dad always said, "If you know better, do better!" It is one thing not to know that your own thoughts could be undermining your well-being. It is another thing altogether to resist change. Thinking your way to a healthy mind-set and higher PF would seem to be an achievable goal, but if you are determined to remain at business as you usual, it is certainly your choice. Just be mindful that it is a choice.

Stop Insisting on Feeling Bad and Get Comfortable with Taking Care of You

I am not suggesting that you breathe intentionally, combat your negative self-talk, or take some time off so you can have three more reasons to tell yourself what you *should* be doing. If all you do is begin saying, "I should breathe more deeply," "I should stop being so negative in my head," "I should be able to take a day off," you have not helped yourself—you have instead guilted yourself. These new skills are hard to implement. That is not your fault.

Perhaps during your first day off, you can find out what is making you uncomfortable with taking care of yourself. Are you simply determined to follow in the footsteps of your mother and grandmother, who worked themselves to the bone? That would be noble. However, do you think that they would have worked themselves to the bone if they did not have to do so? Do they (or did they) have all the resources that you have? If you hold their superhuman achievements as your ideal, you may need to make some adjustments in how you are seeing yourself— for the sake of yourself.

Start by seeing how you expend extra energy that you do not have by putting yourself down. When your coworker seems to ignore you at the coffee shop, taking a deep breath will help you assume that she did not see you instead of launching into a huge storyline with bad feelings and wasted energy. This is not easy work if you are in a perpetual state of negative self-talk, but you can begin somewhere. And shoulding her or you is like building yourself up by two feet only to knock yourself down by six. Absolutely nothing is accomplished.

When you use your breathing skills, check your thinking, and dismiss your shoulds, you gain a reinforced tool belt for handling life stress. Sometimes stress can get to you before you know it, but you can survive the bad feelings that come with stress if you are prepared. In fact, some situations will feel more manageable.

There are some realities that are in your control and some that are not. In a perfect world, you would be able to avoid situations that stress you out all the time, but there are some that you simply cannot avoid. Consider your elderly aunt whom you care for. Her favorite word in the whole dictionary is "should." In fact, you think she should not use should as much as she does. Her criticisms drive you nuts: "You should never have divorced that man." "You should never have married him in the first place." "You should whoop your son because back in my day, children knew how to act." "You should dress better." "You shouldn't spend so much money on your children." "You should cook and not eat out so much."

She relies on you, but she is relentless. You cannot tell her that she should shut up (though you do in your head). You might need to learn to limit how much of your psychological fortitude you sacrifice to your aunt. It already starts to decrease a little bit as you turn down the street to her house, so do whatever you need to bring yourself into the moment.

As I describe my own strategy, think of one behavior you can start cultivating.

When I have a situation that keeps me from saying what I want to say because to do so would be disrespectful, I make sure that I have a fresh pack of my favorite peppermint gum on hand. I keep gum with me for work and also when I am writing. For me, there is something about chewing a piece of gum that allows me to reset and get my head in the game. It's not a perfect solution, but I don't need perfection. I just need to chew and pop gum until the moment is over and so I don't say something that will make a situation worse. Gum seems to give me the outlet I need so I can see that, despite how tired and disgusted I might be, the person who is shoulding on me probably has lower psychological fortitude than I do. As Michelle Obama famously said, "When they go low, we must go high." If I need a piece of gum to help with the liftoff, I'll take it.

If you forget your gum, feel free to take a time-out. Excuse yourself to the restroom for a few minutes to do your deep breathing. Unless your little ones are with you, no one will follow you there. The goal is to do whatever you need to do to remove yourself mentally from a stressful moment and limit the chances that you will say something that you cannot take back.

You Are Worth the Effort

Recognize also that nothing is simple. I decided to look up the definition of "simple"—not because I did not know what it meant but because I did not want to oversell the idea. "Simple" means to be easily understood or easily done. The synonyms are problematic when it comes to your ability to use my proposed psychological fortitude tools. The synonyms for simple are: "straightforward," "easy," "uncomplicated," "effortless." Not one of these applies to what you will have to do. I mentioned earlier in the chapter that these tools might appear to be deceptively simple because anyone can apply them and they don't require complicated steps. While I have no doubt that you can understand the task before you, I expect that you will encounter some challenges and you will have to put in a fair amount of effort.

If you could have already changed on your own, you would have. Though the tools may be straightforward to understand, they are not easy. It's time to get to work, but part of the reason that you may not be ready is because of what you are telling yourself. The things that you tell yourself are unhelpful.

I have said this before, and I'll repeat it: there are things that are in your control, and there are things that are out of your control. This is important for you to realize. People who are anxious often worry about things that are out of their control. They create unnecessary worry and fear. Your time is much better spent focused on the things that are in your control. You working long hours is in your control. You may say that it is not and that you must work long hours and get four hours of sleep per night so you can get the promotion. If you are happy, go for it. If you are not, you have some decisions to make to reclaim control of your work life.

Your Mind Is Your Most Powerful Tool

It's true that your mind works in powerful ways to shape your life. It's a tool you already have and a huge part of what you can and cannot change. It is the powerful tool that affects your decisions and how you feel about what you think you do and what you actually do. Your mind is what you will reclaim. It is already yours, but you forfeited your rights to it in exchange for attention, love, or a nice car to match your upwardly mobile dream. You gave it away so you would be accepted into the right organizations, so you could get a promotion, so you could marry the right person, or so you would not be alone. No matter your age or stage of life, it is not too late to make some changes and reclaim what is yours.

Has anyone ever told you that you were too smart for your own good? If you heard this when you were a teenager or younger adult, you don't hear it anymore. Everything seems to have worked out in your favor. You are making good money, supporting yourself and your daughter, and maybe even supporting the naysayers too. All of your success does not mean that you are not still getting in your own way. Just because no one has told you in a while that you are too smart for your own good does not mean that you have everything figured out. It just means that they do not know your internal struggles. They do not see how hard you work to keep everything balanced and in order even when you are tired of being tired.

I recently talked to one friend about "shoulding" on herself. She was so moved by the idea that she immediately jumped into action with ending the practice despite my warning of trying to notice the habit first. Like me and you, she is an overachiever. As you know, no one has time to observe when you can act. After a week, she told me that she found different ways to imply should without actually saying should. It was awesome. She acknowledged that she knew what she was doing. In one way or another, she was still noticing her behavior even if she was simultaneously finding ways around the intended goal.

When I was in graduate school, one of my wise supervisors told me that time is God's way of keeping things from happening all at once. It was a profound statement that stuck with me over the years. It happened to fit with my favorite scripture that everything happens in its season. Programs such as Alcoholics Anonymous that support those who struggle with alcoholism have twelve steps for a reason. We cannot be successful at step two without mastering step one. We have to diagnose problems before we jump in with interventions. Otherwise, the outcome can be quite frustrating because we work so hard but with no plan for addressing the real problem.

Would you work out, put on fresh clothes, and then shower? You may skip steps at work on occasion, but not when it matters and not on a regular basis. Take the time for you to figure out what you need rather than jumping to uninformed conclusions. You cannot successfully reclaim your mind while skipping steps. Recognize that you are reclaiming the mind of your mother and your grandmother and your great-great-great-grandmother. It does not end there. You are reclaiming your mind for your daughter and for her sons and daughters. They will have to do some reclaiming, but they will have less to do rather than stumbling into it as you may have done when someone gave you this book.

Find ways to begin with small steps. Place handy reminders to yourself with sticky notes on your laptop or alerts on your phone. There are a number of motivational memes and inspiring ideas that suggest ways for you to use positive thinking rather than negative self-talk. I have a decorative pillow that reminds me to "live, love, and laugh." I also have a card from a friend that I framed. It says to "wake up each day and tell the world to bring it!" You may remind yourself that you can do all things through Christ who strengthens you. This one from Maya Angelou is so very relevant for what we've talked about here: "If you don't like something, change it. If you can't change it, change your attitude."[41]

This chapter will not end all of your problems, but it will get you on your way to a more positive mind-set. There are so many things that you cannot change in your life, but if you can change something that is frustrating for you, do it. If you cannot, get a piece of peppermint gum and hang on.

CHAPTER 12

Claiming Your Truths Makes Change Possible

Having high culturally reinforced psychological fortitude does not mean that you will not have low and difficult times in life. Everyone struggles with something at some point in life. Psychological fortitude is not about that "Strong Black Woman" persona that you, your friends, and your family think so highly of in the midst of difficult times. Your Strong Black Woman persona—who gives of herself to everything and everyone—presents as if nothing is ever wrong and can handle anything that is thrown at her. This persona is not your psychological fortitude. This persona weakens your PF.

Embracing an artificial version of psychological fortitude drives you to overeat your way to an early grave and disregard your emotional well-being and your physical health all in the name of looking like you have everything together. No one would say that you died by suicide, but when you repeatedly make poor decisions that impact your health, it is a self-inflicted wound. Make a decision to take control of your PF and your life.

There is no substitute for confronting your life challenges head-on in the same way that there is no substitute for real sugar. If you prefer sweet tea, like my southern sistren, neither the blue nor the pink packet of artificial sweetener will do. You cannot achieve an acceptable level of psychological fortitude with a fake, inauthentic you. What is authenticity? According to the Merriam-Webster dictionary, the authentic or real you "conforms to the original" and "is true to [your] own spirit/personality," not "imitation." If you do not nurture the real you, with all of your imperfections, past failures, and different texture of hair in the front and back, you will stifle your ability to be your best self. You will stifle your talents and gifts because your fortitude is spent on overmanaging your façade. Have you ever called someone "fake" or "phony"? Did you like that person? We most value those who keep it real no matter what.

One of my favorite authentic people to follow on Instagram is Tracee Ellis Ross. She seems to live her best life—with or without makeup, hair done or not, silliness abound or more silliness. I do not know her personally, but I doubt that her confidence to live this life happened overnight but instead grew over time.

If you have been living someone else's life, I would not expect for you to achieve high PF overnight either. If you have been immersed in the myth of strong womanhood, you can at least begin to be honest with yourself. It would seem to take a lot of extra work to keep up appearances, and who has time for that? Think about your favorite strong Black woman-friend. She may actually have psychological fortitude that is equal to 65. She is working hard to hide all of the ways that she is frustrated with her life while simultaneously not addressing the cause of her distress. Are there qualities about yourself that you can and want to change? Good. Create a plan for change rather than beating yourself up over why things are the way that they are.

Even though I know what people mean when they refer to me as a strong Black woman, I do not buy into the myth. I have accomplished more than most at this stage of life—Black or not, woman or not. But my accomplishments do not keep me from feeling overwhelmed at times. After I have a good cry and regroup, I take an honest look at what is going on. I try to figure out what I am doing that is not working. Am I on the right path? Have I taken on too much because of what I "should" be doing? Am I fighting a fight that I was supposed to let God fight for me while I sit still? Is there someone that I can ask for help? My success does not preclude me from asking for help when I need it. It is rarely easy for me to ask for help, but I try to tell myself two things, especially when I am least inclined to ask for help:

1. I can struggle over something for days or ask someone else who can move it along in an hour or less.

2. I would want someone to ask me for help if they truly needed it and I could help. I would feel bad if they didn't ask. Instead, I can give someone an opportunity to help and maybe, just maybe, they will ask me when they need me!

One day, I would like for us to be able to talk about our psychological fortitude and how it is genuinely at 80 to 90 on most days and 50 on other days. We can acknowledge that there are days that are harder than others, but that we know the tough days are temporary. If we ever feel that it is not temporary, we will reach out to someone else rather than binge on chips and cookies.

The Daily Choice to Cultivate Psychological Fortitude

Instead of slowing down, you stress out over having too much to do, not having things go your way, and eventually feeling like you are just going through the motions of life rather than living life. If you are overwhelmed and simultaneously wondering what your purpose is in life, you may need to regroup.

Throughout this book, I have offered alternatives to pressing through as if nothing gets to you. Try them as something different, and especially do these things to expand your true fortitude:

- Be honest that you are overwhelmed and have more on your plate than you can manage. Do not "press through" as you typically do.

- Take control by skipping an event, canceling a commitment, or calling in to work. Use the time to come up with a game plan for what absolutely needs to get done and what you can remove from your plate permanently.

- Be okay with saying no and canceling when you need to do so. Because no one knows what you are going through but you, you are the only one who has to approve of your cancellation. Guilty feelings are not necessary and will undermine your psychological fortitude (or trick you into not taking the day off from work).

- You need the downtime to regroup and to do something for you: pick up lunch for yourself, go to the movies, get a manicure, sit quietly on your back patio for fifteen or forty minutes. You cannot continue to overextend yourself while simultaneously failing to reinvest in your own well-being.

- Do not spend time in your head ruminating about how your life is not going your way. Rethinking negative thoughts without a concrete plan for your next steps will feel worse because you won't actually accomplish anything.

- If you need a different perspective on a frustrating situation or on how overwhelmed you feel, text a friend. She may be at work, but ask when she has twenty minutes to chat.

- Pray—and pray specifically for what you need to do or not do. Be patient for an answer. It will show up like a thought you never had or as unexpected advice that sounds perfect. If the idea or advice takes you outside your comfort zone, then great. It may be time to stretch yourself to something new.

- Give yourself space to have good days and bad days. Trouble does not last always. If you can get through a tough time on your own, great. If you need help, call someone you trust. If she cares about you, she will be okay if you say, "I cannot talk about everything that is going on, but I need someone to sit with for a little while or get happy hour."

Ignore the Naysayers and Look Past Stigma

You probably know someone who would tell you that things aren't that bad. Skeptics will argue that the experts are lying about suicide statistics and that the reported rates are intended to create false alarm. In response to an online article that I was interviewed for, a reader responded, "and water is wet," when I noted that racism may be partly to blame for the increase in suicide for Black children. I do not think that the reader aimed to diminish my point. Sometimes I wonder if we criticize statistical reports and minimize our mental distress as an excuse to do nothing. It is an excuse that feeds your helplessness and the notion that things aren't that bad, so you don't have to do anything differently.

It's my opinion that if one Black person dies by suicide that could have been prevented, that is one too many. If you can glean any kernels of truth from this book that will increase your ability to enjoy more of your life (or enjoy your life at all) after years of feeling like you've just been going through the motions, then it's worth it to pay attention to what I'm saying.

I know the naysayers are not in the majority, but they can throw a whole wrench in a very productive conversation. I sometimes find myself checking the comments sections of articles where I have been cited so I can keep my finger on the pulse of these conversations. Insert one misinformed comment and the whole discussion is derailed or abruptly ends.

So don't be discouraged by naysayers. You can choose to engage them with the new understanding that you gain from this text, or you can conclude for yourself that they are fearful and not ready to do things differently. That does not make them wrong or combative. They're just not where you are. This is worth repeating to keep you from getting dragged into a useless argument: "They are not wrong or ignorant or angry or any of those negative labels. They are simply not where I am." You can move forward with new approaches to living your life and taking care of your family without being distracted by those who are stuck in doing things the way that they have always been done.

Our community has a long history and a devoted relationship with stigma, denial, and shame when it comes to health and emotional health issues. Behind the proud belief that we are a strong people is a practiced habit of hiding our illnesses and struggles, explaining away the troubling behaviors of our loved ones, and suffering our secrets in silence. Stigma is this unbelievable force in our community that says you cannot get help. If you are real about it, stigma says there is no problem. I do think that we are seeing a decrease in the power of stigma, but the decrease is moving at a glacial pace.

Stick to What You Witness and Boost What You've Got

The shame that you have about how truly overwhelmed you are can be a very real barrier to attaining the relief that you seek. If you suspect that you have a problem with anxiety or depression, you might have become very adept at ignoring this about yourself and pushing through. You may be embarrassed that your son has been thinking of suicide because you feel that you have failed as a mother. Yes, you went to college. Yes, you are smart. But I doubt seriously that you were ever taught how to deal with anxiety and depression the way that you learned to diagram a sentence, solve a differential equation, or even pass the state bar exam.

To recognize low psychological fortitude in yourself or in others, you cannot be in denial, you cannot be the frog in the pot, and you cannot get stuck behind the stigma train. Perhaps you can do more to take a "detour" around stigma and shame, especially when you see it in people around you. They may try to discourage you from seeing and doing things differently. Maybe you are the source of the stigma. Maybe you tell yourself that because you are so "strong," you should not have to call in reinforcements.

It is time to do something different, make a different kind of decision—for yourself, for your children, for your nieces and nephews, and for generations of Black people to come. Recognize that there could be a problem for which there is no right or wrong answer, just a different response than your typical choice. After reading this book, you have options. You are now on a path to navigate a limited system and create your own system until new offerings come online...and in case they never do.

Acknowledgments

What I know more than anything is that I am grateful for each and every individual family member, friend, co-conspirator, university colleague, and New Harbinger Publications collaborator who was dispatched on an earthly mission to get me to this stage of life and completion of this book. My journey has made more sense because of your enthusiasm and/or guidance.

I am most grateful for my momma, Rebecca G. Walker, for giving me life and for her many sacrifices so that I could indeed do anything that I put my mind to doing. My daddy, Wilbur Walker, departed this life too soon, but I was tremendously blessed to know his sense of humor, to share his endless curiosity, and to have him as my biggest fan.

Thank you, Kristie, my "baby sister," who I can always count on no matter what. I appreciate that you get more excited about my accomplishments than I do. I am also truly grateful for my big sister and brother, Michelle and Steve, and my brothers-in-law, Cliff and Benjamin, who I can count on for support and timely jokes. Thank you, Aunt Cynthia (Neely) for *always* checking on me. You, Sonja, Uncle Reggie, and Jaxson are the extended family that everybody needs. I am grateful to be a product of all of my extended families—the Germans, the Rivers, and the Graham-Hursts.

I am blessed to have sista-friends who have been in my life for as few as five and as many as thirty-five years. Thank you, Stacy Davis Stanton, Sagdrina Jalal, Chanel Phillips, and Devoyce Gray for reading and providing feedback on earlier drafts of the book. I am grateful also for Tassandra Allen, Dr. Tracey Weldon-Stewart, Dr. Qiana Whitted, and Professor Jacinda Townsend, who provided me with much-needed input.

Thank you to Deb McMillan Kai Kai, Dr. Tenaya Watson, Dr. Edelyn Verona, Dr. Shawn Utsey, Buu Willis, Maisha Cutter, Dr. Yolanda Johnson, Dr. Lisa Richardson, Stephanie Dixon, Dr. Leslie

Bessellieu, Dr. Amanda Rolle, Sharita Robinson, Rose Campbell, Kai Brown-Lang, Dr. Kevin Cokley, and Dr. Gigi Awad for friendship that has been there just when I needed it. Special shout-out also to my "academic peeps" and my current and former doctoral students whom I have been fortunate to have as collaborators.

Through no effort of my own, I have always stumbled into the right people and places at the right time. My own spiritual growth has taken flight under the preaching and convictive teaching of Rev. Dr. Marcus D. Cosby, senior pastor at Wheeler Avenue Baptist Church in Houston, Texas. I am so grateful to be a "Wheelerite" and also indebted to Rev. Dr. Barbara Williams and Rev. Regina Allen for sharing their thoughts on religious references in the book.

I would be remiss if I did not thank Dr. Na'im Akbar, a true visionary who is the reason that I embrace African psychology for Black people. Thank you for being an inspiration to me and to countless others. Many thanks also to Dr. Thomas Joiner Jr. for being an invaluable mentor and trusting me in the 1990s to begin the Black suicide research that made sense to me. I wouldn't be here if you hadn't included me in your first cohort of "Joinerites."

My writing consultant, Gina Carroll, is heaven-sent. There is no other way to explain her ability to communicate my own thoughts to me as easily as she does. I am blessed to know Gina. I am also immensely grateful for my acquisitions editor, Ryan Buresh. Thank you, Ryan, for your confidence in me since day one. It has meant the world seeing this project through to the end. The collaboration with you, Jennifer Holder, Gretel Hakanson, and the New Harbinger team is truly remarkable.

Last but certainly not least, I am grateful for my two special guys. This book is possible because my very patient hubbie, Dr. Ezemenari Obasi, who supports me when I'm out of steam and keeps everything afloat. Thank you for your sacrifice. And thank you, Kamau, for choosing me to be your mom. I promise to do my best so you also know that you can do anything you set your mind to achieve. I can't wait for the adventure that awaits you.

Notes

Chapter 1

1   Bridge, J. A., et al. 2015. "Suicide Trends Among Elementary School-Aged Children in the United States From 1993 to 2012." *JAMA Pediatrics* 169, no. 7: 673–677.

2   Bridge, J. A., et al. 2018. "Age-Related Racial Disparity in Suicide Rates Among US Youths from 2001 through 2015." *JAMA Pediatrics* 172, no. 7: 697–699.

3   Guthrie, R. V. 2004. *Even the Rat Was White: A Historical View of Psychology*. New York: Pearson Education.

4   Early, K. E., and Akers, R. L. 1993. "It's a White Thing: An Exploration of Beliefs About Suicide in the African-American Community." *Deviant Behavior* 14, no. 4: 277–296.

5   Silverman, M. M., et al. 2007. "Rebuilding the Tower of Babel: A Revised Nomenclature for the Study of Suicide and Suicidal Behaviors Part 2: Suicide-Related Ideations, Communications, and Behaviors." *Suicide and Life-Threatening Behavior* 37, no. 3: 264–277.

6   Office of the Surgeon General. US Department of Health and Human Services. 2001. *Report of a Surgeon General's Working Meeting on the Integration of Mental Health Services and Primary Health Care*. Rockville, MD: Office of the Surgeon General. Available from https://www.ncbi.nlm.nih.gov/books/NBK44335/

7   Walker, R. L., Lester, D., and Joe, S. 2006. "Lay Theories of Suicide: An Examination of Culturally Relevant Suicide Beliefs and Attributions Among African Americans and European Americans." *Journal of Black Psychology* 32, no. 3: 320–334.

8   Walker, R. L., et al. 2018. "Religious Coping Style and Cultural Worldview Are Associated with Suicide Ideation Among African American Adults." *Archives of Suicide Research* 22, no. 1: 106–117.

Chapter 2

9   Hoffman, K. M., et al. 2016. "Racial Bias in Pain Assessment and Treatment Recommendations, and False Beliefs About Biological Differences Between Blacks and Whites." *Proceedings of the National Academy of Sciences* 113, no. 16: 4296–4301.

10   Mossey, J. M. 2011. "Defining Racial and Ethnic Minorities in Pain Management." *Clinical Orthopaedics and Related Research* 469, no. 7: 1859–1870.

11   Doran, G. T. 1981. "There's a S.M.A.R.T. Way to Write Management's Goals and Objectives." *Management Review* 70, no. 11: 35–36.

12   Joiner, T. E., Jr., et al. 1999. "Scientizing and Routinizing the Assessment of Suicidality in Outpatient Practice." *Professional Psychology: Research and Practice* 30, no. 5: 447.

Chapter 3

13   Centers for Disease Control and Prevention. "Leading Causes of Death by Age Group, Black Males–United States, 2015." https://www.cdc.gov/healthequity/lcod/men/2015/black/index.htm.

14   Wolfgang, M. E. 1959. "Suicide by Means of Victim-Precipitated Homicide." *Journal of Clinical & Experimental Psychopathology* 30: 335–349.

Chapter 4

15   Gorman, J. M. 1996. "Comorbid Depression and Anxiety Spectrum Disorders." *Depression and Anxiety* 4, no. 4: 160–168.

16   Bor, J., et al. 2018. "Police Killings and Their Spillover Effects on the Mental Health of Black Americans: A Population-Based, Quasi-Experimental Study." *The Lancet* 392, no. 10144: 302–310.

17   American Psychiatric Association. 2013. *Diagnostic and Statistical Manual of Mental Disorders (DSM-5)*. Philadelphia: American Psychiatric Association.

18   Perilla, J. L., Norris, F. H., and Lavizzo, E. A. 2002. "Ethnicity, Culture, and Disaster Response: Identifying and Explaining Ethnic Differences in PTSD Six Months After Hurricane Andrew." *Journal of Social and Clinical Psychology* 21, no. 1: 20–45.

19   Bor, J., et al. 2018. "Police Killings and Their Spillover Effects on the Mental Health of Black Americans: A Population-Based, Quasi-Experimental Study." *The Lancet* 392, no. 10144: 302–310.

20   Baker, F. M. 2001. "Diagnosing Depression in African Americans." *Community Mental Health Journal* 37, no. 1: 31–38. https://doi-org.ezproxy.lib.uh.edu/10.1023/A:1026540321366.

Chapter 5

21   See for example, "H&M Apologises Over Image of Black Child in 'Monkey' Hoodie," *The Guardian*, January 8, 2018. https://www.theguardian

.com/fashion/2018/jan/08/h-and-m-apologises-over-image -of-black-child-in -monkey-hoodie.

22   Washington, H. A. 2006. *Medical Apartheid: The Dark History of Medical Experimentation on Black Americans from Colonial Times to the Present.* New York: Doubleday Books.

23   Schulz, A. J., et al. 2006. "Discrimination, Symptoms of Depression, and Self-Rated Health Among African American Women in Detroit: Results from a Longitudinal Analysis." *American Journal of Public Health* 96, no. 7: 1265–1270.

24   Walker, R. L., et al. 2014. "Perceived Racism and Suicide Ideation: Mediating Role of Depression but Moderating Role of Religiosity Among African American Adults." *Suicide and Life-Threatening Behavior* 44, no. 5: 548–559.

25   Baldwin, J., et al. 1961. "The Negro in American Culture." *Cross Currents* 11, no. 3: 205–224. http://www.jstor.org/stable/24456864.

26   Williams, D. R., et al. 2007. "Prevalence and Distribution of Major Depressive Disorder in African Americans, Caribbean Blacks, and Non-Hispanic Whites: Results from the National Survey of American Life." *Archives of General Psychiatry* 64, no. 3: 305–315.

27   Guthrie, R. V. 2004. *Even the Rat Was White: A Historical View of Psychology.* New York: Pearson Education.

28   Goff, P. A., et al. 2008. "Not Yet Human: Implicit Knowledge, Historical Dehumanization, and Contemporary Consequences." *Journal of Personality and Social Psychology* 94, no. 2: 292.

29   Maarifacircle. 2018. "Dr. Asa Hilliard III—The Science of Racism." YouTube video, 7:57. December 8. https://www.youtube.com/watch?v=0J1XyBr0iaI.

Chapter 7

30   Hilliard, A. 1988. "Free Your Mind, Return to the Source: African Origins." Transcript. East Point, GA: Waset Educational Productions.

31   Du Bois, W. E. B. 1909. "Evolution of the Race Problem," in *Proceedings of the National Negro Conference.* New York: s. n., 142–158.

32   Hilliard, A. G., III. 1998. *SBA: The Reawakening of the African Mind.* Gainesville, FL: Makare Publishing Company.

33   Williams, D. R., et al. 2007. "Prevalence and Distribution of Major Depressive Disorder in African Americans, Caribbean Blacks, and Non-Hispanic Whites: Results from the National Survey of American Life." *Archives of General Psychiatry* 64, no. 3: 305–315.

Chapter 8

34   Sahgal, N., and Smith, G. 2009. "A Religious Portrait of African Americans." Pew Research Center. (January 30.) http://www.pewforum.org/2009/01/30/a-religious-portrait-of-african-americans.

35   Mattis, J. S. 2000. "African American Women's Definitions of Spirituality and Religiosity." *Journal of Black Psychology* 26, no. 1: 101–122.

36   Scriven, J. 1855. "What a Friend We Have in Jesus." Originally published by Scriven anonymously as a poem and later composed as a hymn by Charles Crozat Converse in 1868.

37   Lorde, A. 2017. *A Burst of Light and Other Essays*. Mineola, NY: Courier Dover Publications.

Chapter 9

38   Selye, H. 1956. *The Stress of Life*. New York: McGraw Hill Education.

Chapter 10

39   National Alliance on Mental Illness. "Finding a Mental Health Professional." https://www.nami.org/Find-Support/Living-with-a-Mental-Health-Condition/Finding-a-Mental-Health-Professional.

Chapter 11

40   Burns, D. D. (1999). *Feeling good: The New Mood Therapy* (Rev. ed.). New York: Avon.

41   Angelou, M. 1994. *Wouldn't Take Nothing for My Journey Now*. New York: Bantam Books.

Rheeda Walker, PhD, is a tenured professor of psychology in the department of psychology at the University of Houston. She is a behavioral science researcher and licensed psychologist who has published more than fifty scientific papers on African American adult mental health, suicide risk, and resilience. Walker is recognized as a fellow in the American Psychological Association due to her scholarly accomplishments.

Walker has been a guest expert psychologist on T.D. Jakes's national television talk show, and her work has appeared or been cited in *The Washington Post*, CNN Health, the *Houston Chronicle*, and *Ebony* magazine. Her expertise has been critical to mentoring doctoral students in cross-cultural psychology since 2003. Walker was previously a lead consultant in the statewide African American Faith-Based Education and Awareness initiative in Texas. She conducts workshops, and coordinates with churches and other organizations to address emotional wellness.

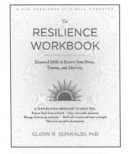

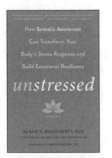